SUMMIT BOOKS
NEW YORK LONDON TORONTO SYDNEY TOKYO

THANK GOD
FOR THE
ATOM BOMB

AND
OTHER ESSAYS

PAUL
FUSSELL

Copyright © 1988 by Paul Fussell
All rights reserved
including the right of reproduction
in whole or in part in any form.
Published by SUMMIT BOOKS
A Division of Simon & Schuster Inc.
Simon & Schuster Building
Rockefeller Center
1230 Avenue of the Americas
New York, NY 10020

SUMMIT BOOKS and colophon are trademarks of
Simon & Schuster Inc.

Designed by SNAP-HAUS GRAPHICS
Manufactured in the United States of America

10   9   8   7   6   5   4   3   2   1

Library of Congress Cataloging in Publication Data

Fussell, Paul.
   Thank God for the atom bomb and other essays.

   I. Title.
AC8.F94   1988   081   88-2234
ISBN 0-671-63866-1

To Harriette

FOREWORD

Looking over these pieces, many of which are about war, I see that they propose another sort of battlefield, where the enemy consists of habitual euphemizers, professional dissimulators, inadequately educated academic administrators, censors, artistically pretentious third-rate novelists, sexual puritans, rigid optimists and Disneyfiers of life, writers who bitch about the reviews they receive, humorless critical doctrinaires with grievances (Marxist, Feminist, what-have-you), the sly rhetoricians of the National Rifle Association, exploiters of tourists, and, of course, the President. In short, this is not a book to promote tranquillity, and readers in quest of peace of mind should look elsewhere.

For invitations to write or speak and for information, suggestions, encouragement, or other benefactions I am indebted to Nancy Aakre, Joseph W. Angell, Richard Barrett, Jack Beatty, Martin Beiser, James Cahill, Arthur Cooper, George Core, Ted Dow, Matthew Evans, Robert Harper, Doris Hatcher, Jennifer Herman, Samuel Hynes, William Jovanovich, John Keegan, Frederick Kiley, Horst Jarka, Henry Kizor, William McGuire, Earl Miner, Margaret Mitchell, John Preston, Steven Rothman, Sergio Ruffini, John Scanlan, Eugene B. Sledge, Michael Walzer, Kay Whittle, and Nancy Wilson Ross. Carleton University, the University of Hong Kong, the Mansfield Foundation of the University of Montana, the Memorial University of Newfoundland, the University of Pennsylvania, and l'Università degli Studi di Perugia have been generous patrons. Many of my observations on the fate of chivalry echo the findings of Theodore Bogacz in *The Journal of Modern History* for September 1986. I am grateful for his perceptions.

Pieces published before have appeared as follows: "Thank God for the Atom Bomb" and "An Exchange of Views," *The New Republic,* August 26–29 and September 23, 1981; "George Orwell: The Critic as Honest Man," *Sewanee Review,* Spring 1985; "Killing, in Verse and Prose," *Boston Globe,* December 2, 1984, and *Chicago Sun-Times,* September 16, 1984; "A Well-Regulated Militia," *The New Republic,* June 27, 1981; "Taking It All Off in the Balkans," *Gentlemen's Quarterly,* April 1987; "Modernism, Adversary Culture, and Edmund Blunden," *Sewanee Review,* Fall 1986; "Indy," *Harper's,* August 1982.

CONTENTS

THANK GOD
FOR THE
ATOM BOMB

Many years ago in New York I saw on the side of a bus a whiskey ad I've remembered all this time. It's been for me a model of the short poem, and indeed I've come upon few short poems subsequently that exhibited more poetic talent. The ad consisted of two eleven-syllable lines of "verse," thus:

In life, experience is the great teacher.
In Scotch, Teacher's is the great experience.

For present purposes we must jettison the second line (licking our lips, to be sure, as it disappears), leaving the first to register a principle whose banality suggests that it enshrines a most useful truth. I bring up the matter because, writing on the forty-second anniversary of the atom-bombing of Hiroshima and Nagasaki, I want to consider something suggested by the long debate about the ethics, if any, of that ghastly affair. Namely, the importance of experience, sheer, vulgar experience, in influencing, if not determining, one's views about that use of the atom bomb.

The experience I'm talking about is having to come to grips, face to face, with an enemy who designs your death. The experience is common to those in the marines and the infantry and even the line navy, to those, in short, who fought the Second World War mindful always that their mission was, as they were repeatedly assured, "to close with the enemy and destroy him." *Destroy,* notice: not hurt, frighten, drive away, or capture. I think there's something to be learned about that war, as well as about the tendency of historical memory unwittingly to resolve ambiguity and generally clean up the premises, by considering the way testimonies emanating from real war experience tend to complicate attitudes about the most cruel ending of that most cruel war.

"What did you do in the Great War, Daddy?" The recruiting poster deserves ridicule and contempt, of course, but here its question is embarrassingly relevant, and the problem is one that touches on the dirty little secret of social class in America. Arthur T. Hadley said recently that those for whom the use of the A-bomb was "wrong" seem to be implying "that it would have been better to allow thousands on thousands of American and Japanese infantrymen to die in honest hand-to-hand combat on the beaches than to drop those two bombs." People holding such views, he notes, "do not come from the ranks of society that produce infantrymen or pilots." And there's an eloquence problem: most of those with firsthand experience of the war at its worst were not elaborately educated people. Relatively inarticulate, most have remained silent about what they know. That is, few of those destined to be blown to pieces if the main Japanese islands had been invaded went on to become our most effective men of letters or impressive ethical theorists or professors of contemporary history or of international law. The testimony of experience has tended to come from rough diamonds—James Jones is an example—who went through the war as enlisted men in the infantry or the Marine Corps.

Anticipating objections from those without such experience, in his book *WWII* Jones carefully prepares for his chapter on the A-bombs by detailing the plans already in motion for the infantry assaults on the home islands of Kyushu (thirteen divisions scheduled to land in November 1945) and ultimately Honshu (sixteen divisions scheduled for March 1946). Planners of the invasion assumed that it would require a full year, to November 1946, for the Japanese to be sufficiently worn down by land-combat attrition to surrender. By that time, one million American casualties was the expected price. Jones observes that the forthcoming invasion of Kyushu "was well into its collecting and stockpiling stages before the war ended." (The island of Saipan was designated a main ammunition and supply base for the invasion, and if you go there today you can see some of the assembled stuff still sitting there.) "The assault troops were chosen and already in training," Jones reminds his readers, and he illuminates by the light of experience what this meant:

What it must have been like to some old-timer buck sergeant or staff sergeant who had been through Guadalcanal or Bougainville or the Philippines, to stand on some beach and watch this huge war machine beginning to stir and move all around him and know that he very likely had survived this far only to fall dead on the dirt of Japan's home islands, hardly bears thinking about.

Another bright enlisted man, this one an experienced marine destined for the assault on Honshu, adds his testimony. Former Pfc. E. B. Sledge, author of the splendid memoir *With the Old Breed at Peleliu and Okinawa,* noticed at the time that the fighting grew "more vicious the closer we got to Japan," with the carnage of Iwo Jima and Okinawa worse than what had gone before. He points out that

what we had *experienced* [my emphasis] in fighting the Japs (pardon the expression) on Peleliu and Okinawa caused us to formulate some very definite opinions that the invasion . . . would be a ghastly bloodletting. . . . It would shock the American public and the world. [Every Japanese] soldier, civilian, woman, and child would fight to the death with whatever weapons they had, rifle, grenade, or bamboo spear.

The Japanese pre-invasion patriotic song, "One Hundred Million Souls for the Emperor," says Sledge, "meant just that." Universal national kamikaze was the point. One kamikaze pilot, discouraged by his unit's failure to impede the Americans very much despite the bizarre casualties it caused, wrote before diving his plane onto an American ship, "I see the war situation becoming more desperate. All Japanese must become soldiers and die for the Emperor." Sledge's First Marine Division was to land close to the Yokosuka Naval Base, "one of the most heavily defended sectors of the island." The marines were told, he recalls, that

> due to the strong beach defenses, caves, tunnels, and numerous Jap suicide torpedo boats and manned mines, few Marines in the first five assault waves would get ashore alive—my company was scheduled to be in the first and second waves. The veterans in the outfit felt we had already run out of luck anyway. . . . We viewed the invasion with complete resignation that we would be killed—either on the beach or inland.

And the invasion was going to take place: there's no question about that. It was not theoretical or merely rumored in order to scare the Japanese. By July 10, 1945, the prelanding naval and aerial bombardment of the coast had begun, and the battleships *Iowa, Missouri, Wisconsin,* and *King George V* were steaming up and down the coast, softening it up with their sixteen-inch shells.

On the other hand, John Kenneth Galbraith is persuaded that the Japanese would have surrendered surely by November without an invasion. He thinks the A-bombs were unnecessary and unjustified because the war was ending anyway. The A-bombs meant, he says, "a difference, at most, of two or three weeks." But at the time, with no indication that surrender was on the way, the kamikazes were sinking American vessels, the *Indianapolis* was sunk (880 men killed), and Allied casualties were running to over 7,000 per week. "Two or three weeks," says Galbraith. Two weeks more means 14,000 more killed and wounded, three weeks more, 21,000. Those weeks mean the world if you're one of those thousands or related to one of them. During the time between the dropping of the Nagasaki bomb on August 9 and the actual surrender on the fifteenth, the war pursued its accustomed course: on the twelfth of August eight captured American fliers were executed (heads chopped off); the fifty-first United States submarine, *Bonefish*, was sunk (all aboard drowned); the destroyer *Callaghan* went down, the seventieth to be sunk, and the Destroyer Escort *Underhill* was lost. That's a bit of what happened in six days of the two or three weeks posited by Galbraith. What did he do in the war? He worked in the Office of Price Administration in Washington. I don't demand that he experience having his ass shot off. I merely note that he didn't.

Likewise, the historian Michael Sherry, author of a recent book on the rise of the American bombing mystique, *The Creation of Armageddon,* argues that we didn't delay long enough between the test explosion in New Mexico and the mortal explosions in Japan. More delay would have made possible deeper moral considerations and perhaps laudable second thoughts and restraint. "The risks of delaying the bomb's use," he says, "would have been small—not the thousands of casualties expected of invasion but only a few days or weeks of relatively routine operations." While the mass murders represented by these "relatively routine operations" were enacting, Michael Sherry was safe at home. Indeed, when the bombs were dropped he was going on eight months old, in danger only of falling out of his pram. In speaking thus of Galbraith and Sherry, I'm aware of the offensive implications *ad hominem*. But what's at stake in an infantry assault is so entirely unthinkable to those without the experience of one, or several, or many, even if they possess very wide-ranging imaginations and warm sympathies, that experience is crucial in this case.

In general, the principle is, the farther from the scene of horror, the easier the talk. One young combat naval officer close to the action wrote home in the fall of 1943, just before the marines underwent the agony of Tarawa: "When I read that we will fight the Japs for years if necessary and will sacrifice hundreds of thousands if we must, I always like to check from where he's talking: it's seldom out here." That was Lieutenant (j.g.) John F. Kennedy. And Winston Churchill, with an irony perhaps too broad and easy, noted in Parliament that the people who preferred invasion to A-bombing seemed to have "no intention of proceeding to the Japanese front themselves."

A remoteness from experience like Galbraith's and

Sherry's, and a similar rationalistic abstraction from actuality, seem to motivate the reaction of an anonymous reviewer of William Manchester's *Goodbye Darkness: A Memoir of the Pacific War* for *The New York Review of Books.* The reviewer naturally dislikes Manchester's still terming the enemy Nips or Japs, but what really shakes him (her?) is this passage of Manchester's:

> After Biak the enemy withdrew to deep caverns. Rooting them out became a bloody business which reached its ultimate horrors in the last months of the war. You think of the lives which would have been lost in an invasion of Japan's home islands—a staggering number of Americans but millions more of Japanese—and you thank God for the atomic bomb.

Thank God for the atom bomb. From this, "one recoils," says the reviewer. One does, doesn't one?

And not just a staggering number of Americans would have been killed in the invasion. Thousands of British assault troops would have been destroyed too, the anticipated casualties from the almost 200,000 men in the six divisions (the same number used to invade Normandy) assigned to invade the Malay Peninsula on September 9. Aimed at the reconquest of Singapore, this operation was expected to last until about March 1946—that is, seven more months of infantry fighting. "But for the atomic bombs," a British observer intimate with the Japanese defenses notes, "I don't think we would have stood a cat in hell's chance. We would have been murdered in the biggest massacre of the war. They would have annihilated the lot of us."

The Dutchman Laurens van der Post had been a pris-
oner of the Japanese for three and a half years. He and
thousands of his fellows, enfeebled by beriberi and pellagra,
were being systematically starved to death, the Japanese ra-
tionalizing this treatment not just because the prisoners were
white men but because they had allowed themselves to be
captured at all and were therefore moral garbage. In the
summer of 1945 Field Marshal Terauchi issued a significant
order: at the moment the Allies invaded the main islands, all
prisoners were to be killed by the prison-camp commanders.
But thank God that did not happen. When the A-bombs
were dropped, van der Post recalls, "This cataclysm I was
certain would make the Japanese feel that they could with-
draw from the war without dishonor, because it would strike
them, as it had us in the silence of our prison night, as
something supernatural."

In an exchange of views not long ago in *The New York Review
of Books,* Joseph Alsop and David Joravsky set forth the by
now familiar argument on both sides of the debate about the
"ethics" of the bomb. It's not hard to guess which side each
chose once you know that Alsop experienced capture by the
Japanese at Hong Kong early in 1942, while Joravsky came
into no deadly contact with the Japanese: a young, combat-
innocent soldier, he was on his way to the Pacific when the
war ended. The editors of *The New York Review* gave the debate
the tendentious title "Was the Hiroshima Bomb Necessary?"
surely an unanswerable question (unlike "Was It Effective?")
and one precisely indicating the intellectual difficulties involved in imposing *ex post facto* a rational and even a genteel
ethics on this event. In arguing the acceptability of the bomb,

Alsop focuses on the power and fanaticism of War Minister Anami, who insisted that Japan fight to the bitter end, defending the main islands with the same techniques and tenacity employed at Iwo and Okinawa. Alsop concludes: "Japanese surrender could never have been obtained, at any rate without the honor-satisfying bloodbath envisioned by . . . Anami, if the hideous destruction of Hiroshima and Nagasaki had not finally galvanized the peace advocates into tearing up the entire Japanese book of rules." The Japanese plan to deploy the undefeated bulk of their ground forces, over two million men, plus 10,000 kamikaze planes, plus the elderly and all the women and children with sharpened spears they could muster in a suicidal defense makes it absurd, says Alsop, to "hold the common view, by now hardly challenged by anyone, that the decision to drop the two bombs on Japan was wicked in itself, and that President Truman and all others who joined in making or who [like Robert Oppenheimer] assented to this decision shared in the wickedness." And in explanation of "the two bombs," Alsop adds: "The true, climactic, and successful effort of the Japanese peace advocates . . . did not begin in deadly earnest until *after* the second bomb had destroyed Nagasaki. The Nagasaki bomb was thus the trigger to all the developments that led to peace." At this time the army was so unready for surrender that most looked forward to the forthcoming invasion as an indispensable opportunity to show their mettle, enthusiastically agreeing with the army spokesman who reasoned early in 1945, "Since the retreat from Guadalcanal, the Army has had little opportunity to engage the enemy in land battles. But when we meet in Japan proper, our Army will demonstrate its invincible superiority." This possibility foreclosed by the Emperor's post-A-bomb surrender broadcast, the shocked, disappointed officers of one infantry battalion, anticipating a professionally impressive defense of the beaches, killed themselves in the following numbers: one major, three captains, ten first lieutenants, and twelve second lieutenants.

David Joravsky, now a professor of history at Northwestern, argued on the other hand that those who decided to use the A-bombs on cities betray defects of "reason and self-restraint." It all needn't have happened, he says, "if the U.S. government had been willing to take a few more days and to be a bit more thoughtful in opening up the age of nuclear warfare." I've already noted what "a few more days" would mean to the luckless troops and sailors on the spot, and as to being thoughtful when "opening up the age of nuclear warfare," of course no one was focusing on anything as portentous as that, which reflects a historian's tidy hindsight. The U.S. government was engaged not in that sort of momentous thing but in ending the war conclusively, as well as irrationally Remembering Pearl Harbor with a vengeance. It didn't know then what everyone knows now about leukemia and various kinds of carcinoma and birth defects. Truman was not being sly or coy when he insisted that the bomb was "only another weapon." History, as Eliot's "Gerontion" notes,

. . . has many cunning passages, contrived corridors
And issues, deceives with whispering ambitions,
Guides us by vanities. . . .
                                        Think

Neither fear nor courage saves us.
   Unnatural vices
Are fathered by our heroism. Virtues
Are forced upon us by our impudent crimes.

Understanding the past requires pretending that you don't know the present. It requires feeling its own pressure on your pulses without any *ex post facto* illumination. That's a harder thing to do than Joravsky seems to think.

   The Alsop-Joravsky debate, reduced to a collision between experience and theory, was conducted with a certain civilized respect for evidence. Not so the way the scurrilous, agitprop *New Statesman* conceives those justifying the dropping of the bomb and those opposing. They are, on the one hand, says Bruce Page, "the imperialist class-forces acting through Harry Truman" and, on the other, those representing "the humane, democratic virtues"—in short, "fascists" as opposed to "populists." But ironically the bomb saved the lives not of any imperialists but only of the low and humble, the quintessentially democratic huddled masses—the conscripted enlisted men manning the fated invasion divisions and the sailors crouching at their gun-mounts in terror of the Kamikazes. When the war ended, Bruce Page was nine years old. For someone of his experience, phrases like "imperialist class forces" come easily, and the issues look perfectly clear.

   He's not the only one to have forgotten, if he ever knew, the unspeakable savagery of the Pacific war. The dramatic postwar Japanese success at hustling and merchandising and tourism has (happily, in many ways) effaced for most people the vicious assault context in which the Hiroshima horror should be viewed. It is easy to forget, or not to know, what Japan was like before it was first destroyed, and then humiliated, tamed, and constitutionalized by the West. "Implacable, treacherous, barbaric"—those were Admiral Halsey's characterizations of the enemy, and at the time few facing the Japanese would deny that they fit to a T. One remembers the captured American airmen—the lucky ones who escaped decapitation—locked for years in packing crates. One remembers the gleeful use of bayonets on civilians, on nurses and the wounded, in Hong Kong and Singapore. Anyone who actually fought in the Pacific recalls the Japanese routinely firing on medics, killing the wounded (torturing them first, if possible), and cutting off the penises of the dead to stick in the corpses' mouths. The degree to which Americans register shock and extraordinary shame about the Hiroshima bomb correlates closely with lack of information about the Pacific war.

And of course the brutality was not just on one side. There was much sadism and cruelty, undeniably racist, on ours. (It's worth noting in passing how few hopes blacks could entertain of desegregation and decent treatment when the U.S. Army itself slandered the enemy as "the little brown Jap.") Marines and soldiers could augment their view of their own invincibility by possessing a well-washed Japanese skull, and very soon after Guadalcanal it was common to treat surrendering Japanese as handy rifle targets. Plenty of Japanese gold teeth were extracted—some from still living mouths—with Marine Corps Ka-Bar knives, and one of E. B. Sledge's fellow marines went around with a cut-off Japanese hand. When its smell grew too offensive and Sledge urged him to get rid of it, he defended his possession of this trophy thus: "How many Marines you reckon that hand pulled the trigger on?" (It's hardly necessary to observe that a soldier in the ETO would probably not have dealt that way with a German or Italian—that is, a "white person's"— hand.) In the Pacific the situation grew so public and scandalous that in September 1942, the Commander in Chief of the Pacific Fleet issued this order: "No part of the enemy's body may be used as a souvenir. Unit Commanders will take stern disciplinary action. . . ."

Among Americans it was widely held that the Japanese were really subhuman, little yellow beasts, and popular imagery depicted them as lice, rats, bats, vipers, dogs, and monkeys. What was required, said the Marine Corps journal *The Leatherneck* in May 1945, was "a gigantic task of extermination." The Japanese constituted a "pestilence," and the only appropriate treatment was "annihilation." Some of the marines landing on Iwo Jima had "Rodent Exterminator" written on their helmet covers, and on one American flagship the naval commander had erected a large sign enjoining all to "KILL JAPS! KILL JAPS! KILL MORE JAPS!" Herman Wouk remembers the Pacific war scene correctly while analyzing Ensign Keith in *The Caine Mutiny:* "Like most of the naval executioners of Kwajalein, he seemed to regard the enemy as a species of animal pest." And the feeling was entirely reciprocal: "From the grim and desperate taciturnity with which the Japanese died, they seemed on their side to believe that they were contending with an invasion of large armed ants." Hiroshima seems to follow in natural sequence:

"This obliviousness of both sides to the fact that the opponents were human beings may perhaps be cited as the key to the many massacres of the Pacific war." Since the Jap vermin resist so madly and have killed so many of us, let's pour gasoline into their bunkers and light it and then shoot those afire who try to get out. Why not? Why not blow them all up, with satchel charges or with something stronger? Why not, indeed, drop a new kind of bomb on them, and on the un-uniformed ones too, since the Japanese government has announced that women from ages of seventeen to forty are being called up to repel the invasion? The intelligence officer of the U.S. Fifth Air Force declared on July 21, 1945, that "the entire population of Japan is a proper military target," and he added emphatically, *There are no civilians in Japan.* Why delay and allow one more American high school kid to see his own intestines blown out of his body and spread before him in the dirt while he screams and screams when with the new bomb we can end the whole thing just like that?

On Okinawa, only weeks before Hiroshima, 123,000 Japanese and Americans *killed* each other. (About 140,000 Japanese died at Hiroshima.) "Just awful" was the comment on the Okinawa slaughter not of some pacifist but of General MacArthur. On July 14, 1945, General Marshall sadly informed the Combined Chiefs of Staff—he was not trying to scare the Japanese—that it's "now clear . . . that in order to finish with the Japanese quickly, it will be necessary to invade the industrial heart of Japan." The invasion was definitely on, as I know because I was to be in it.

When the atom bomb ended the war, I was in the

Forty-fifth Infantry Division, which had been through the
European war so thoroughly that it had needed to be recon-
stituted two or three times. We were in a staging area near
Rheims, ready to be shipped back across the United States
for refresher training at Fort Lewis, Washington, and then
sent on for final preparation in the Philippines. My division,
like most of the ones transferred from Europe, was to take
part in the invasion of Honshu. (The earlier landing on Kyushu was to be carried out by the 700,000 infantry already in
the Pacific, those with whom James Jones has sympathized.)
I was a twenty-one-year-old second lieutenant of infantry
leading a rifle platoon. Although still officially fit for combat,
in the German war I had already been wounded in the back
and the leg badly enough to be adjudged, after the war, 40
percent disabled. But even if my leg buckled and I fell to the
ground whenever I jumped out of the back of a truck, and
even if the very idea of more combat made me breathe in
gasps and shake all over, my condition was held to be ade-
quate for the next act. When the atom bombs were dropped
and news began to circulate that "Operation Olympic"
would not, after all, be necessary, when we learned to our
astonishment that we would not be obliged in a few months
to rush up the beaches near Tokyo assault-firing while being
machine-gunned, mortared, and shelled, for all the practiced
phlegm of our tough façades we broke down and cried with
relief and joy. We were going to live. We were going to
grow to adulthood after all. The killing was all going to be
over, and peace was actually going to be the state of things.
When the _Enola Gay_ dropped its package, "There were
cheers," says John Toland, "over the intercom; it meant the

end of the war." Down on the ground the reaction of
Sledge's marine buddies when they heard the news was more
solemn and complicated. They heard about the end of the
war

> with quiet disbelief coupled with an indescribable sense
> of relief. We thought the Japanese would never surren-
> der. Many refused to believe it. . . . Sitting in stunned
> silence, we remembered our dead. So many dead. So
> many maimed. So many bright futures consigned to the
> ashes of the past. So many dreams lost in the madness
> that had engulfed us. Except for a few widely scattered
> shouts of joy, the survivors of the abyss sat hollow-eyed
> and silent, trying to comprehend a world without war.

These troops who cried and cheered with relief or who sat
stunned by the weight of their experience are very different
from the high-minded, guilt-ridden GIs we're told about by
J. Glenn Gray in his sensitive book *The Warriors.* During the
war in Europe Gray was an interrogator in the Army Coun-
terintelligence Corps, and in that capacity he experienced the
war at Division level. There's no denying that Gray's outlook
on everything was admirably noble, elevated, and responsible.
After the war he became a much-admired professor of philosophy at Colorado College and an esteemed editor of Hei-
degger. But *The Warriors,* his meditation on the moral and
psychological dimensions of modern soldiering, gives every
sign of error occasioned by remoteness from experience.
Division headquarters is miles—*miles*—behind the line

where soldiers experience terror and madness and relieve those pressures by crazy brutality and sadism. Indeed, unless they actually encountered the enemy during the war, most "soldiers" have very little idea what "combat" was like. As William Manchester says, "All who wore uniforms are called veterans, but more than 90 percent of them are as uninformed about the killing zones as those on the home front." Manchester's fellow marine E. B. Sledge thoughtfully and responsibly invokes the terms *drastically* and *totally* to underline the differences in experience between front and rear, and not even the far rear, but the close rear. "Our code of conduct toward the enemy," he notes, "differed drastically from that prevailing back at the division CP." (He's describing gold-tooth extraction from still-living Japanese.) Again he writes: "We existed in an environment totally incomprehensible to men behind the lines . . . ," even, he would insist, to men as intelligent and sensitive as Glenn Gray, who missed seeing with his own eyes Sledge's marine friends sliding under fire down a shell-pocked ridge slimy with mud and liquid dysentery shit into the maggoty Japanese and USMC corpses at the bottom, vomiting as the maggots burrowed into their own foul clothing. "We didn't talk about such things," says Sledge. "They were too horrible and obscene even for hardened veterans. . . . Nor do authors normally write about such vileness; unless they have seen it with their own eyes, it is too preposterous to think that men could actually live and fight for days and nights on end under such terrible conditions and not be driven insane." And Sledge has added a comment on such experience and the insulation provided by even a short distance: "Often people just behind our rifle companies couldn't understand what we knew." Glenn Gray was not in a rifle company, or even just behind one. "When the news of the atomic bombing of Hiroshima and Nagasaki came," he asks us to believe, "many an American soldier felt shocked and ashamed." Shocked, OK, but why ashamed? Because we'd destroyed civilians? We'd been doing that for years, in raids on Hamburg and Berlin and Cologne and Frankfurt and Mannheim and Dresden, and Tokyo, and besides, the two A-bombs wiped out 10,000 Japanese troops, not often thought of now, John Hersey's kindly physicians and Jesuit priests being more touching. If around division headquarters some of the people Gray talked to felt ashamed, down in the rifle companies no one did, despite Gray's assertions. "The combat soldier," he says,

> knew better than did Americans at home what those bombs meant in suffering and injustice. The man of conscience realized intuitively that the vast majority of Japanese in both cities were no more, if no less, guilty of the war than were his own parents, sisters, or brothers.

I find this canting nonsense. The purpose of the bombs was not to "punish" people but to stop the war. To intensify the shame Gray insists we feel, he seems willing to fiddle the facts. The Hiroshima bomb, he says, was dropped "without any warning." But actually, two days before, 720,000 leaflets were dropped on the city urging everyone to get out and indicating that the place was going to be (as the Potsdam Declaration has promised) obliterated. Of course few left.

Experience whispers that the pity is not that we used the bomb to end the Japanese war but that it wasn't ready in time to end the German one. If only it could have been rushed into production faster and dropped at the right moment on the Reich Chancellery or Berchtesgaden or Hitler's military headquarters in East Prussia (where Colonel Stauffenberg's July 20 bomb didn't do the job because it wasn't big enough), much of the Nazi hierarchy could have been pulverized immediately, saving not just the embarrassment of the Nuremberg trials but the lives of around four million Jews, Poles, Slavs, and gypsies, not to mention the lives and limbs of millions of Allied and German soldiers. If the bomb had only been ready in time, the young men of my infantry platoon would not have been so cruelly killed and wounded.

All this is not to deny that like the Russian Revolution, the atom-bombing of Japan was a vast historical tragedy, and every passing year magnifies the dilemma into which it has lodged the contemporary world. As with the Russian Revolution, there are two sides—that's why it's a tragedy instead of a disaster—and unless we are, like Bruce Page, simple-mindedly unimaginative and cruel, we will be painfully aware of both sides at once. To observe that from the viewpoint of the war's victims-to-be the bomb seemed precisely the right thing to drop is to purchase no immunity from horror. To experience both sides, one might study the book *Unforgettable Fire: Pictures Drawn by Atomic Bomb Survivors,* which presents a number of amateur drawings and watercolors of the Hiroshima scene made by middle-aged and elderly survivors for a peace exhibition in 1975. In addition to the almost unbearable pictures, the book offers brief moments of memoir not for the weak-stomached:

> While taking my severely wounded wife out to the river bank . . . , I was horrified indeed at the sight of a stark naked man standing in the rain with his eyeball in his palm. He looked to be in great pain but there was nothing that I could do for him. I wonder what became of him. Even today, I vividly remember the sight. I was simply miserable.

These childlike drawings and paintings are of skin hanging down, breasts torn off, people bleeding and burning, dying mothers nursing dead babies. A bloody woman holds a bloody child in the ruins of a house, and the artist remembers her calling, "Please help this child! Someone, please help this child. Please help! Someone, please." As Samuel Johnson said of the smothering of Desdemona, the innocent in another tragedy, "It is not to be endured." Nor, it should be noticed, is an infantryman's account of having his arm blown off in the Arno Valley in Italy in 1944:

> I wanted to die and die fast. I wanted to forget this miserable world. I cursed the war, I cursed the people who were responsible for it, I cursed God for putting me here . . . to suffer for something I never did or knew anything about.

(A good place to interrupt and remember Glenn Gray's noble but hopelessly one-sided remarks about "injustice," as well as "suffering.")

"For this was hell," the soldier goes on,

> and I never imagined anything or anyone could suffer so bitterly. I screamed and cursed. Why? What had I done to deserve this? But no answer came. I yelled for medics, because subconsciously I wanted to live. I tried to apply my right hand over my bleeding stump, but I didn't have the strength to hold it. I looked to the left of me and saw the bloody mess that was once my left arm; its fingers and palm were turned upward, like a flower looking to the sun for its strength.

The future scholar-critic who writes *The History of Canting in the Twentieth Century* will find much to study and interpret in the utterances of those who dilate on the special wickedness of the A-bomb-droppers. He will realize that such utterance can perform for the speaker a valuable double function. First, it can display the fineness of his moral weave. And second, by implication it can also inform the audience that during the war he was not socially so unfortunate as to find himself down there with the ground forces, where he might have had to compromise the purity and clarity of his moral system by the experience of weighing his own life against someone else's. Down there, which is where the other people were, is the place where coarse self-interest is the rule. When the young soldier with the wild eyes comes at you, firing, do you shoot him in the foot, hoping he'll be hurt badly enough to drop or mis-aim the gun with which he's going to kill you, or do you shoot him in the chest (or, if you're a prime shot, in the head) and make certain that you and not he will be the survivor of that mortal moment?

It would be not just stupid but would betray a lamentable want of human experience to expect soldiers to be very sensitive humanitarians. The Glenn Grays of this world need to have their attention directed to the testimony of those who know, like, say, Admiral of the Fleet Lord Fisher, who said, "Moderation in war is imbecility," or Sir Arthur Harris, director of the admittedly wicked aerial-bombing campaign designed, as Churchill put it, to "de-house" the German civilian population, who observed that "War is immoral," or our own General W. T. Sherman: "War is cruelty, and you cannot refine it." Lord Louis Mountbatten, trying to say something sensible about the dropping of the A-bomb, came up only with "War is crazy." Or rather, it requires choices among crazinesses. "It would seem even more crazy," he went on, "if we were to have more casualties on our side to save the Japanese." One of the unpleasant facts for anyone in the ground armies during the war was that you had to become pro tem a subordinate of the very uncivilian George S. Patton and respond somehow to his unremitting insistence that you embrace his view of things. But in one of his effusions he was right, and his observation tends to suggest the experiential dubiousness of the concept of "just wars." "War is not a contest with gloves," he perceived. "It is resorted to only when laws, which are rules, have failed." Soldiers being like that, only the barest decencies should be expected of them. They did not start the war, except in the terrible sense hinted at in Frederic Manning's observation based on his front-line experience in the Great War: "War is waged by men; not by beasts, or by gods. It is a peculiarly human activity. To call it a crime against mankind is to miss at least half its significance; it is also the punishment of a crime." Knowing that unflattering truth by experience, soldiers have every motive for wanting a war stopped, by any means.

The stupidity, parochialism, and greed in the international mismangement of the whole nuclear challenge should not tempt us to misimagine the circumstances of the bomb's first "use." Nor should our well-justified fears and suspicions occasioned by the capture of the nuclear-power trade by the inept and the mendacious (who have fucked up the works at Three Mile Island, Chernobyl, etc.) tempt us to infer retrospectively extraordinary corruption, imbecility, or motiveless malignity in those who decided, all things considered, to drop the bomb. Times change. Harry Truman was not a fascist but a democrat. He was as close to a genuine egalitarian as anyone we've seen in high office for a long time. He is the only President in my lifetime who ever had experience in a small unit of ground troops whose mission it was to kill people. That sort of experience of actual war seems useful to presidents especially, helping to inform them about life in general and restraining them from making fools of themselves needlessly—the way Ronald Reagan did in 1985 when he visited the German military cemetery at Bitburg containing the SS graves. The propriety of this visit he explained by asserting that no Germans who fought in the war remain alive and that "very few . . . even remember the war." Reagan's ignorance or facile forgetfulness are imputed by Arthur Schlesinger to his total lack of serious experience of war—the Second World War or any other. "Though he often makes throwaway references to his military career," says Schlesinger, "Mr. Reagan in fact is the only American president who was of military age during the Second World War and saw no service overseas. He fought the war on the film lots of Hollywood, slept in his own bed every night and apparently got many of his ideas of what happened from subsequent study of the *Reader's Digest*."

Truman was a different piece of goods entirely. He knew war, and he knew better than some of his critics then and now what he was doing and why he was doing it. "Having found the bomb," he said, "we have used it. . . . We have used it to shorten the agony of young Americans."

The past, which as always did not know the future, acted in ways that ask to be imagined before they are condemned. Or even simplified.

AN EXCHANGE
OF VIEWS

(from *The New Republic,* September 23, 1981)

PAUL FUSSELL's defense of the bombing of Hiroshima is written, as he tells us repeatedly, from the standpoint of the ordinary GI. And that standpoint is human, all too human: let anyone die but me! There are no humanitarians in the foxholes. I can almost believe that. But Fussell's recital does remind me a little uneasily of the speech of that Conradian villain Gentleman Brown (in *Lord Jim*): "When it came to saving one's life in the dark, one didn't care who else went—three, thirty, three hundred people. . . ." And Brown went on to boast, very much as Fussell wants to do, that he made Jim wince with this "despairing frankness": "He very soon left off coming the righteous over me. . . ."

But we shouldn't be intimidated, and we shouldn't leave off, but accept the risks of righteousness. After all, Fussell's argument isn't only the argument of ordinary soldiers. It is also and more importantly the argument of ordinary generals—best expressed, I think, by the Prussian general von Moltke in 1880: "The greatest kindness in war is to bring it to a speedy conclusion. It should be allowable, with that end in view, to employ all means save those that are absolutely objectionable." But von Moltke, a stolid professional, probably still believed that the wholesale slaughter of civilians was "absolutely objectionable." With Fussell, it seems, there are no limits at all; anything goes, so long as it helps to bring the boys home.

Nor is this the argument only of GIs and generals. The bombing of Hiroshima was an act of terrorism; its purpose was political, not military. The goal was to kill enough civilians to shake the Japanese government and force it to surrender. And this is the goal of every terrorist campaign. Happily, none of today's terrorist movements have yet been able to kill on the scale of the modern state, and so they have not enjoyed successes as dramatic as the one Fussell describes. But their ordinary members, the terrorists in the foxholes, as it were, must think much as he does: if only we could kill enough people, not a dozen here and there, in a pub, a bus station, or a supermarket, but a whole city full, we could end the struggle once and for all, liberate our land, get the British out of Ireland, force the Israelis to accept a PLO state, and so on. To the boys of the IRA, to young Palestinians in Lebanon, that argument is surely as attractive as it was to the young Paul Fussell on his way to the Pacific in 1945. It is the same argument.

What is wrong with it? If war is indeed a tragedy, if its suffering is inevitable, then nothing is wrong with it. War is war, and what happens, happens. In fact, however, war imposes choices on officers and enlisted men alike. "There wasn't a single soldier," says an Israeli officer who fought in the Six-Day War, "who didn't at some stage have to decide, to choose, to make a moral decision. . . ." Fussell, who has written so beautifully about the literature of war, must know this to be true. And he must also know that there is a moral argument, different from his own argument, that shapes these military choices. Perhaps that argument is most often expounded by those professors far from the battlefield for whom he has such contempt. But it is an argument as old as war itself and one that many soldiers have believed and struggled to live by. It holds, most simply, that combat should be a struggle between combatants, and that noncombatants—civilian men, women, and children—should be protected as far as possible against its cruelties. "The soldier, be he friend or foe," wrote Douglas MacArthur, "is charged with the protection of the weak and the unarmed. It is the very essence and reason of his being . . . a sacred trust." Like policemen, firemen, and sailors at sea, soldiers have a responsibility to accept risks themselves rather than impose risks on ordinary citizens. That is a hard requirement when the soldiers are conscripts. Still, they are trained and armed for war and ordinary citizens are not; and that is a practical difference that makes a moral difference.

Consider how the risks of police work might be reduced, and how many more criminals might be caught, if we permitted the police to ignore the rights of ordinary citizens, to fire indiscriminately into crowds, to punish the innocent relatives of criminals, and so on. But we don't grant such permissions. Nor are soldiers permitted comparable acts, even if they carry with them the promise of success.

There is a code. It is no doubt often broken, particularly in the heat of battle. But honorable men live by it while they can. Hiroshima was a violation of that code. So was the earlier terror bombing of cities—Hamburg, Dresden, Tokyo —but Hiroshima was worse because it was even more terrifying. Its long-term effects were literally unknowable by the men who decided to impose them. And the effects were not imposed, any more than those of the earlier bombing, in the heat of battle, face-to-face with enemy soldiers who aim to kill and have already killed comrades and friends. Though there were soldiers in Hiroshima, they were not the targets of the attack (or else we would have attacked a military base); the city was the target and all its inhabitants.

Fussell writes (again) as a democrat, on behalf of "the low and humble, the quintessentially democratic huddled masses—the conscripted enlisted men manning the fated invasion divisions." Given that standpoint, one might have expected him to question the U.S. demand for unconditional surrender that made the invasion of the Japanese islands seem absolutely necessary. There were people in the U.S. government in 1945 who thought a negotiated settlement possible without an invasion and without the use of the atomic bomb. Surely some attempt should have been made—not only for the sake of our own soldiers, but also for those other "huddled masses," the civilian inhabitants of Hiroshima (and Nagasaki too). Why don't they figure in Fussell's democratic reckoning! If Harry Truman's first responsibility was to American soldiers, he was not without responsibility elsewhere; no man is. And if one is reckoning, what about all the future victims of a politics and warfare from which restraint has been banished? Given the state of our political and moral order, with which Hiroshima probably has something to do, aren't we all more likely to be the victims than the beneficiaries of terrorist attacks?

MICHAEL WALZER

author of *Just and Unjust Wars: A Moral*
Argument with Historical Illustrations (1977)

I'm grateful to Michael Walzer for his courteous demurrer, but I think we're never going to agree, for our disagreement is one between sensibilities. I'd designate them as, on the one hand, the ironic and ambiguous (or even the tragic, if you like), and, on the other, the certain. The one complicates problems, leaving them messier than before and making you feel terrible. The other solves problems and cleans up the place, making you feel tidy and satisfied. I'd call the one sensibility the literary-artistic-historical; I'd call the other the social-scientific-political. To expect them to agree, or even to perceive the same data, would be expecting too much.

My aim in writing the article on Hiroshima was to

complicate, even mess up, the moral picture. What Walzer does in his comment by playing on our anxieties, with terms like "terrorist" anachronistically applied, is to simplify it again. I was saying that I was simultaneously horrified about the bombing of Hiroshima and forever happy because the event saved my life. Both at the same time. I'll stick with William Blake:

Under every grief & pine
Runs a joy with silken twine.

I don't want to dispute data, but I think Walzer's not right when he says: "Though there were soldiers in Hiroshima, they were not the targets of the attack (or else we would have attacked a military base)." But Hiroshima was a military base, the headquarters of the Japanese Second Army, and the soldiers were the target of the attack: we dropped the bomb accurately on the corner of their parade ground and killed thousands of them. But our disagreement is not really about such facts, but about two different emotional and moral styles. If Michael Walzer thinks the "huddled masses" of Hiroshima and Nagasaki don't figure in my reckoning, he's not read carefully. It is because they do figure that I dwelt on the pathos and horror registered so touchingly in *Unforgettable Fire.* And because I don't think right-eousness all on one side, I also dwelt on the deeper pathos and horror of the war's continuing. Walzer says of the bomb-dropping that its purpose was political, not military. I say that its purpose was political and military, sadistic and humanitarian, horrible and welcome.

My object was to offer a soldier's view, to indicate the complex moral situation of knowing that one's life has been saved because others' have been most cruelly snuffed out. I was arguing the importance of combat experience, alas, in influencing one's views on the ethics of the bomb. I observed that those who deplore the dropping of the bomb absolutely turn out to be largely too young to have been killed if it hadn't been used. I don't want to be needlessly offensive, nor to insist that no person whose life was not saved by the A-bomb can come to a clear—by which I mean a complicated —understanding of the moral balancesheet. But I note that in 1945 Michael Walzer, for all the emotional warmth of his current argument, was ten years old.

PAUL FUSSELL

POSTSCRIPT (1987)
ON
JAPANESE SKULLS

When *The New Republic* first published "Hiroshima: A Soldier's View" (the original title of the preceding essay) a great deal of mail came in, more, the editor said, than from any article he remembered. Most of the letters were from elderly survivors of the Pacific war, ex-marines and ex-infantrymen, and they cheered themselves hoarse. But one former marine did not: he objected to my point that a much-envied wartime trophy among members of the Marine Corps was a well-washed Japanese skull. "The charge is preposterous," he said. "I was a private in the Marine infantry on Tulagi, Guadalcanal, Roi-Namur, and Saipan. In the course of the war I served with the First, Second, and Fourth Marine Divisions. I never saw or heard of such a practice."

This ex-marine's innocence invites four possible explanations: (1) He was remarkably careless in his notice of what was going on. Or (2) he was more intimate with the affairs of the typing pool well back of the line than with what was going on up front. Or (3) decently brought up and a nice person, he decided to See No Evil. Or (4) his memory, anxious like so many people's to cleanse the past, deceives him.

Visiting a friend a few years ago who had been a marine on Guadalcanal, I said I was doing some writing about the Second World War and would welcome a look at any artifacts he might have preserved. It took no more than thirty seconds for him to leap up, fetch a shoebox of snapshots, and bring forth several depicting Japanese skulls serving as trophies and totems on Guadalcanal. One was displayed atop a pole, like a warning at the entrance of a "native village" in a jungle film of the 1930s. Another was mounted on the front of a ruined Japanese tank, looking forward like a radiator ornament of the period. Another was not yet ready for display but was being processed. It was being boiled in a metal vat, and two marines were busy poking it and turning it with sticks. One of these marines was my host, and forty years ago, when the picture was taken, he was a boy, looking as innocent as Holden Caulfield or Jackie Cooper.

It was by no means an "atrocity" that these photo-

Robert Harper

Robert Harper

graphs were recording. They were taken out of pride, like the photos of hanged partisans snapped at the same time a world away by Wehrmacht soldiers. Both kinds of pictures were taken to record proud achievements. They were evidence of how well the respective troops had accomplished their mission, which was to "Kill Him Before He Kills You." The snapshots of the Japanese skulls were taken (and preserved for a lifetime) because the marines were proud of their success in humiliating, punishing, and finally destroying an enemy who, violating a quiet American Sunday, had dared bomb Pearl Harbor, thus inaugurating the marines' prolonged misery by seeking to terminate in maximum agony their brief, unspent lives.

My friend assured me that securing and preserving Japanese skulls was by no means a rare practice and that it had started on Guadalcanal, at the virtual beginning of the ghastly fighting in the Pacific. Because the marines had not yet learned the full depths of Japanese ruthlessness, this early skull-taking seems to register less a sinking of the United States Marine Corps to the Japanese level of brutality—that would come later—than a simple 1940s American racial contempt. Why have more respect for the skull of a Jap than for the skull of a weasel, a rat, or any other form of mad, soulless vermin?

For the ground troops, boiling a skull was a good way to start preserving it for display. Any flesh surviving the boiling was removed by lye. Sailors could cleanse their trophies by running a line through them or placing them in a small net and dragging them for some time behind their vessels, later scrubbing them with lye and strong laundry soap. This is the technique specified in a wartime poem, once quite well known, Winfield Townley Scott's "The U.S. Sailor with the Japanese Skull." This fictional (but true) sailor got his skull also on Guadalcanal. He hacked off the head of a Japanese body he found on the beach there, skinned it, and then gave it the salt-water-immersion treatment until it was fit to be held on his flattened hand and gazed at, producing the effect of a sailor-boy Hamlet considering not his child-hood friend but a detested enemy.

It was a sailor also who was the kind donor of the famous Japanese skull "found on New Guinea" and sent in 1943 as a souvenir to his girlfriend in Phoenix, Arizona. *Life* magazine featured the girl meditating pensively on the skull in a full-page photograph, thus bringing to its several million patriotic readers the good news about Japanese skulls being collected in the Pacific. It's notable that the girl in the pho-tograph is neither a ghoul nor a tramp. She is conspicuously decent and middle class. She is dressed in a nice suit and tasteful earrings, with her blond hair worn up. The photog-rapher has posed her at a desk where she is said to be writing a thank-you note to her generous boyfriend. Perhaps she is answering his message, which he has written in ink on the top of the skull. The tone of both photo and caption is one of calm normality, without a trace of irony or outrage. Charles Lindbergh, on Bougainville in 1944 as a naval aviation consultant, is also quite unexcited when he notes a number of Japanese skulls "set up on posts" along a road being constructed by army engineers. Lindbergh is not at all an exaggerator or an unobjective observer, and he records this not uncommon sight with total dispassion.

My ex-marine correspondent who "never saw or heard of such a practice" seems to have missed knowledge available

Ralph Crane, Black Star

to all in the *Atlantic* for February 1946. There, the war correspondent Edward L. Jones reminded Americans, much too inclined to forget unpleasant facts, of the savagery and madness of the war just ended. He wrote,

We shot prisoners in cold blood, wiped out hospitals, strafed lifeboats, killed or mistreated enemy civilians, finished off the enemy wounded, tossed the dying into a hole with the dead, and in the Pacific boiled the flesh off enemy skulls to make table ornaments for sweethearts, or carved their bones into letter-openers.

If his awareness of skulls and sweethearts seems to derive from *Life,* his allusion to letter-openers recalls a well-known incident where a serviceman in the Pacific sent President Roosevelt a nice gift, a letter-opener carved from a Japanese soldier's thighbone. This the President, or someone in his office, had the delicacy to decline.

Finally, the skeptical ex-marine could clear up the matter in dispute by consulting Bill D. Ross's *Iwo Jima* (1986). This detailed account of the battle ends with a description of a memorial occasion celebrated in 1985 at Camp Pendleton, California, by 400 Marine Corps survivors of Iwo. Ross was present and so was a Buddhist priest from Japan, formerly a captain in the Japanese Navy who supervised the construction of many of the defenses on the island. One of this priest's current duties is presiding over the Association of Iwo Jima, composed of relatives of the 22,000 Japanese killed there. Hearing that Ross was writing a book about the battle, the priest asked for a most important favor. On his many postwar trips back to Iwo, he said, "he had found," Ross reports, "that the skulls of many Japanese killed in battle had been severed from skeletons and, presumably, had been sent or carried back to the States as souvenirs." Given the occasion, the priest was courteous enough to suggest that not the marines but the cleanup troops following them were the culprits. This "puzzled" Ross, he says, for during his research for his book, he had heard, he admits, "of such desecrations elsewhere in the Pacific war." Regardless, Ross is happy to report the priest's appeal:

I appeal to you to plead with anyone who has the skull of a Japanese from Iwo Jima . . . to return the same to me so that I can return them to the island, where, in the name of humanity and the honor of warriors, they belong and can rest in eternal peace.

So if you or your relatives have a skull, or know anyone who has kept one, please send it back to

The Reverend Tsunezo Wachi,
President, Association of Iwo Jima,
2-24-23 Higashicho, Kichijoji,
Musashinoshi, Tokyo, Japan, 180.

WRITING IN WARTIME: THE USES OF INNOCENCE

A really successful war, a psychologically Good War, requires not merely the extirpation of a cruel enemy abroad. It requires as a corollary the apotheosis of the pure of heart at home. In that way the Second World War was even a Better War than we may remember. Let me explain.

A while ago I was at the Imperial War Museum in London, gathering material for a book about the "culture" of the Second World War—that is, everything defining its intellectual, artistic, and psychological atmosphere. I was reading numerous published and unpublished memoirs and diaries and letters and autobiographies in search of a style of personal testimony about traumatic events unique to that war, a style of recall unprecedented in the Great or any other war. I was hoping to perceive and define a particular style in which Second World War writers rendered the ghastly material in their memories into understandable and thus conventional received plots, rhetorical figures, traditional idioms, and clichés. My encounters with such materials from the First World War had made it clear that without such conventional crutches, remembrance, at least remembrance transmissible to others, is not possible.

One of the items I came upon was a little book of ninety-five pages titled *My Sister and I: The Diary of a Dutch Boy Refugee,* published in January 1941, by Harcourt, Brace in New York, at a moment when Britain was disastrously at war but America was not. Five months after it appeared in the United States, the book was published in London, by Faber and Faber. This little book presents the diary of a twelve-year-old Dutch boy, to whom the publishers gave the pseudonym Dirk van der Heide to protect his relatives and friends still in Holland at the time. On the title page the translator of the diary into English is designated as Mrs. Antoon Deventer.

Dirk's diary registers his perceptions and feelings during the German invasion of Holland in May 1940, and it deals especially with the bombing of Rotterdam, one of the first flagrant assaults upon unarmed civilians during the war. The dive-bombing of Rotterdam by German Stukas, which destroyed 20,000 buildings and killed almost a thousand people, was at its time the most destructive air raid ever conducted, and one historical reference work has called it "one of the symbolic acts of the war. Coming while negotiations for surrender were under way," it goes on, "it seemed to represent Nazi wantonness and terrorism at its worst. . . ."

Dirk has lived in the southern suburbs of Rotterdam, and he has been in a position to provide a vivid, if preadolescent and thus innocent, eyewitness account, which reveals him as an extraordinarily bright and sensitive child. He is described by Mrs. Deventer in her Introduction:

> Dirk van der Heide is a sturdy Dutch boy with straight taffy-colored hair that falls over his forehead, mild blue eyes, and a smile that quickly lights up his rather solemn face. . . .

She goes on to indicate Dirk's literary method:

> Dirk has added to the diary since he left Holland. The English captain on the boat that brought Dirk to America could read Dutch, and persuaded him to write his experiences in more detail. He did so without self-consciousness; it is certain that Dirk himself has no realization of how remarkable and how significant his diary really is.

Mrs. Deventer then considers the contribution of the young diarist's innocence to the attractiveness of his work, and she interprets his performance thus:

It is clear to anyone who reads this diary that Dirk is a remarkable boy. Sometimes his writing seems abnormally mature, and sometimes plainly the statement of a healthy and naive child. For us, the message of the diary is in its simple statements, and the humor, courage, and pathos which we can read into it.

And finally Mrs. Deventer posits Dirk as an exemplary moral type-figure, whom she designates "the bewildered child in wartime":

Here the bewildered child in wartime is revealed with a direct force and clarity. This revelation restores faith in the strength of innocence under the worst kind of fire.

In the book which the English ship captain has persuaded Dirk to make of his diary, the lad sets forth his family situation briskly. His father, a veterinarian, was mobilized at the start of the war and is presumably still in Holland, although now, clearly, captured, disarmed, and demobilized by the Germans. When the German invasion started, Dirk's mother went off to volunteer her services at a nearby hospital. His Uncle Pieter has helped him and his nine-year-old sister Keetje escape, finally, to England. "Uncle Pieter," Dirk reports, "hates the Germans for what they are doing to our country and to all the other little countries."

Dirk begins his diary on May 7, 1940. He notices Dutch soldiers everywhere, overhears news of canceled leaves, puzzles over a hurriedly printed government pamphlet titled "What to Do": maintain blackout, disconnect the gas, fill bathtubs, stay off the streets, prepare shelters. Three days later he writes: "Something terrible happened last night. War began!!!" Rotterdam, he reports, has been bombed all day, and he and others in his neighborhood have cowered in an underground shelter maintained by a local baron. The tone prevailing there is a rare "democratic" decency and sympathy: in the shelter, Dirk attests, "People are all very kind to each other and friendly, even the ones who don't speak to each other usually." And Dirk is himself a model of gentleness and sympathy: when a nearby house is hit and its owner and his daughter killed, Dirk comments instinctively, "Poor people." Everyone is scared, including the baron's animals, terrified by the rumbling and shaking, and people are anxious about the rumors of German paratroops descending in the costumes of Dutch clerics.

The next day brings no relief. "The war didn't stop," says Dirk, "but got worse everywhere." So many antiaircraft shell fragments are now dropping from the sky that being outdoors at all is hazardous. "A few people," Dirk writes, "have tin or steel helmets like the soldiers but I wore a kettle over my head and so did many other people." A German leaflet dropped from the air assures its readers that the Germans "come as friends and they were sorry to be doing what they were doing but they had to protect us from the English and the French." This, says Dirk, "made everyone laugh at first and made them angry too." Dirk soon discovers that his own street has been bombed and one of his friends killed, and when Uncle Pieter goes off to the hospital to check on

Dirk's mother, "He didn't find mother," Dirk writes, "because she is dead." And he is barely able to add: "I can't sleep or write anymore now or anything." To add to the horror, that night two old people in the shelter die. "They were not hit by bombs," Dirk says. "They just died."

The next day Uncle Pieter manages to get Dirk and Keetje away, into the safer countryside. He is aiming for the riverside town of Dordrecht, where he hopes to find a boat. But they don't get there easily. The road their car is traveling, swarming with their fellow refugees, is strafed by German planes, and Dirk is inducted into one of the main recurring experiences of anyone living in the twentieth century, helplessly watching the wounded suffer. "Several people were hit," he says. "One woman in front of us, a young woman, sat by the roadside holding her head and groaning. There was blood coming out of her head and a hole in the side. It made me sick. About fifty people were wounded and many were killed." From this episode Dirk concludes that "The Germans are cowards to shoot people who have no guns."

Uncle Pieter presses on and finally secures spaces on a boat departing for England. But they are still not safe. Zigzagging through mines, the vessel in front of theirs is blown up and sunk. Dirk comments: "This war is terrible. It kills just about everybody." No wonder he's glad, as he says, to be "going to England where it will be quiet." And he adds: "I hope the Germans don't come there the way they did in Holland." Uncle Pieter, Dirk, and Keetje finally land at Harwich and soon arrive in London, where at the rail station they find "Many English people . . . to give us breakfast and to help us." After what they've endured, the scene they find in England is almost "pastoral"—the only emotions apparent are kindness, sympathy, and cheerfulness, all exercised with notable self-abnegation. As Dirk reports of the British, "They were all very cheerful and smiling."

But before he and his sister can board a ship at Liverpool that will take them to the United States, Keetje falls ill. Of the British physician who treats her, Dirk says, "He was very kind. He wouldn't let Uncle Pieter pay him anything. He said it was his pleasure and his gift to gallant Holland." Once aboard the ship, Dirk finds the English captain as kind, decent, and cheerful as all the other English he's met. He is "a nice man . . . and is always making jokes." Arriving finally in New York, Dirk and Keetje are met by an uncle and aunt, and are soon enjoying their American school, as well as films and ice-cream sodas and other wonders. Now, says Dirk, "Keejte seems very happy. Sometimes I think she has forgotten about Mother entirely. But I haven't."

As I read this the first time, I was moved and instructed by Dirk's narrative, and finding in it much evidence of the stylistic uniqueness I was looking for, I took copious notes. But gradually I began to feel uneasy. Something odd was going on. It wasn't just that the Germans were depicted as instinctive strafers of unarmed civilians while the Dutch and the British were presented as wholly fine and heroic: you get that in all wartime writing. Nor was it the oddity of the book's being written by a child of considerable literary talent who apparently never wrote anything again: such curious things have happened before. What was really teasing was the book's being written by a twelve-year-old Dutch boy anxious to portray as Good Samaritans, noble in every way, not so much his own people as the British. Why, one couldn't help wondering? A crucial clause that nowadays couldn't help triggering some suspicion was, as it were, thrown away, positioned as the mere second element in a compound sentence near the end of the book. "I hate to leave England," says Dirk. "I have had a good time here and —" (and here's the kicker) "—I hope the Germans never do to England what they did to Holland." At this point, few readers in 1941 could refrain from unconsciously adding a sentence of their own: "But the Germans certainly will do to England what they did to Holland if the United States doesn't get into the war fast and help England defend herself." The reader whose suspicions have been aroused will now realize that as propaganda, Dirk's diary can't help the Dutch, as it pretends to—they are already past help. It can help only the British.

When Dirk's book was published in New York it confounded Harcourt, Brace's sales predictions. The first printing was of 7,500 copies, of which only 6,000 were bound. But by the end of the first year sales had reached over 46,000, and by the time *My Sister and I* finally went out of print, in July 1948, it had sold over 52,000 copies. The vision of innocence under vicious assault delivered by Dirk's narrative was so welcome that the book was generally credited with being what it seemed to be. "An authentic document," the *Christian Century* found it. "An honest child speaks."—M. L. Becker, in *Books.* "The most moving document that has yet come out of the war," said Olga Owens of the *Boston Transcript.* (Olga Owens seems to have had recourse to that old trick of lazy reviewers, appropriating the jacket blurb, which proclaims *My Sister and I* "the most moving document that has come out of the war." The jacket continues: "Only the mind of a boy could record events in the purity of their immediate impact. And only a boy who has seen destruction come to the quiet families of an ordinary town could give a local habitation and a name to war's impersonal terror.") In England as well almost all reviewers fell into line, accepting without reservation the book's claims and enjoying particularly its image of childish innocence struggling to preserve its purity in an adult world made viler than usual by German evil. "As a faithful record of modern warfare in all its horror," said the *Manchester Evening News,* "this slim volume is worth more than many of the big books men and women have compiled in the effort to tell the terrible truth about mass murder and madness. . . . With dispassionate simplicity, exceptional intelligence, and natural humor, [Dirk van der Heide] relates exactly what happened in a story that deserves to be read by all who are still striving to preserve a world fit for other children to be born in." The *Irish Times* agreed that the very childishness of the narrator was one of the book's values, saying, "Far more moving than anything that an older and more experienced man could write." The young author's innocence was celebrated likewise by *John O'London's: "My Sister and I* is especially valuable for this reason: the writer, naturally, has no preconceived malice, no national or political hatreds." And Dirk's objectivity as an infantine *tabula rasa* was found by a writer for *Books of the Month* to give the book special value for ultimate historiography.

To be sure, there were a couple of skeptical voices.

(There always are such killjoys around, avid to spoil other people's simple literary pleasures.) But disbelief was notably quiet and genteel, as if "the war effort" must on no account be impaired, even ever so mildly. Edward Weeks, writing in *The Atlantic Monthly,* did register some doubts about the book's genuineness but hastened to draw on a quasi-Aristotelian understanding of the probable impossibility and the resulting "general truth" of fiction to validate the book in its own way. He wrote: "Whether you take it with or without salt, the horror . . . must be true." And in the London *Times Literary Supplement* a reviewer said that, although Dirk did doubtless write most of the book, "one feels that it has been edited by a more mature hand." But no doubts about Dirk's sole authorship were entertained by Wilhelmina, Queen of the Netherlands, at that time in exile with her retinue in Canada. She spent lots of time urging her courtiers to locate the brave boy author so that she could decorate him. To those who began to suspect that Dirk might be hard to find, the popular Dutch writer Hendrik Willem van Loon, domiciled in the United States, at dinner parties coyly declined either to confirm or deny that he was the real author. The publisher Alfred Knopf—certainly no dummy—was one of many who believed that it was really van Loon's hand that had wielded little Dirk's pen.

Before long, with that easy competence of Americans at shifting the matter of one genre into quite another, Tin Pan Alley seized on Dirk's title and plot and came up with the song "My Sister and I," the title page of whose sheet music read, "As inspired by the current best-seller *My Sister and I,* by Dirk van der Heide." This song was immensely popular during the summer of 1941. I remember its being rendered at an evening entertainment at a yacht club of the period, sung with impressive emotional effect by a twelve-year-old boy soprano, son of one of the proud members. In his little blue blazer and long white duck trousers, he sang (and there was not a dry eye in the house),

My sister and I recall the day
We said goodbye and sailed away;
And we think of our friends who had to stay—
But we don't talk about that.

The last line, an oft-repeated refrain in the song, proved a gift to the lewd and coarse young Americans soon to be corralled into the army of the United States. At one southern training camp, the troops distilled the song into a brisk mock-incestuous version, thought comically appropriate to family life in the southern states. The soldiers sang:

My sister and I—
But we don't talk about that.

Both the real song and the real book, one realizes, were of great value to the British cause in 1941, when Wendell Willkie and Charles Lindbergh were engaged in heated debate about whether the United States should go to war and save the British or stay at peace and let them sink. Because the war ended so satisfyingly a few years later, it's not easy to recall the isolationist atmosphere in 1940 and 1941. While the draft bill was being debated in Congress in 1940, Senator Claude Pepper, one of the bill's enthusiasts, was hanged in effigy at the Capitol by the Congress of American Mothers. The next year hordes of college students organized themselves into an ironic organization called Veterans of Future Wars, and a pamphlet arguing that *The Yanks Are Not Coming* sold 300,000 copies. In that context, it's not terribly hard now, at this distance, to perceive that *My Sister and I* might really be a fairly subtle job of black propaganda. By black, I mean covert: the book, while pretending that it is willing to be understood as a Dutch propaganda gesture, might seem to be rather a shrewd British propaganda maneuver. Such sleight-of-hand would be clearly above the capacity of any twelve-year-old of any nationality. Such skill could suggest only a fully adult master—mistress?—of duplicity, someone like an artist if not in the actual employ of British intelligence, then one close enough to it to do its virtual bidding. Impressed by the professionalism of the author of *My Sister and I,* I set to work to find out as much as I could about the book.

Since I was in London, I first went to Faber & Faber and asked a friend there if, in the interests of literary history, I might take a look at the file on the book. My friend found the file all right, but he found also that it had been thoroughly sanitized, all evidence of the book's authorship having been removed and presumably destroyed. Later, back in New York, I approached Harcourt, Brace (now Harcourt, Brace, Jovanovich) and encountered there a fact even more suggestive. There, the whole file relating to *My Sister and I* had been removed and apparently, as we say since Watergate et al., deep-sixed. And my authoritative Harcourt, Brace informant, as astonished as I was, declared this incident unique: the records of no other book published by that firm had ever disappeared.

I now began to hope that out in the great world there was someone once connected with the book who, since these events occurred over forty-five years ago, perhaps wouldn't mind shedding some light on Dirk van der Heide and his performance. Without entertaining much hope, I inserted "author's queries" in the standard literary outlets—*The New York Times Book Review, The New York Review of Books,* the *Times Literary Supplement*—asking for information about the composition and publication of *My Sister and I.* Deep in my subconscious, I suppose, was Chauncey B. Tinker's good luck with a somewhat similar situation back in 1920. He was about to finish his edition of James Boswell's letters, and hoping at the last moment to uncover a few more letters in private hands, he made his need known in a letter to the *Times Literary Supplement.* After a period of silence, back came the portentous message, scribbled anonymously on a postcard, "Try Malahide Castle." And what he uncovered there was the treasure of Boswell's immense literary archive, for almost two centuries thought destroyed. To compare small things with moderate-sized things, I hoped for a similarly informative response to my query.

An astonishing number of people answered, and some from as far away as Australia. But most had either old or irrelevant news to tell. One wanted me to know that he

possessed a copy of the book. Another said that he had read
My Sister and I in 1941 and had enjoyed it very much. Several
told me they'd never heard of the book but knew the song
derived from it, and they told me about that. But finally—
pay dirt, my version of "Try Malahide Castle." I received a
letter from a man telling me to write a Mrs. Stanley Young,
living in New York State. Had she composed *My Sister and I*,
I wondered, as I wrote asking her what she knew and what
she might be willing to tell. Meanwhile, a woman who was
working in the advertising department of Harcourt, Brace in
1941 wrote me some hints about this affair, saying, "Most of
the actors in that comedy of errors are dead, but there are, I
believe, relatives still alive and capable of kicking who might
prefer to have the little hoax left buried." But when she
finally answered, Mrs. Stanley Young (the novelist Nancy
Wilson Ross) proved not to be one of these. *My Sister and I*,
she revealed, had been written by her late husband—he died
in 1975—while he was working at Harcourt, Brace as an
editor.

Stanley Preston Young was his name. Born in 1906, he
became one of those bright young writers of the 1930s who
worked for newspapers and magazines and publishers and
wrote with equal ease poems, novels, and plays, all good
enough to be published—and the plays professional enough
to run for a while on Broadway—but none impressive
enough for libraries to preserve or literary people to remember. The Stanley Youngs of the period worked on the International *Herald Tribune* or the *New York Times,* and they often
ended in the classier New York publishing houses. Today,
such young men would probably aim for something related

to the stock market, or perhaps a career in law. In Young's time they helped sustain the second level, if it may be called that, of verbal culture. Stanley Young came from Indiana. He graduated from the University of Chicago, took an MA in English at Columbia, and afterward polished himself a bit at Grenoble and Munich. After teaching English for a while at Williams College, he settled finally in publishing and became the managing editor of the Bollingen Series and later managing director of the publishing house of Farrar, Straus. He lived in Westport, Connecticut, whence he commuted, and he told some close friends once that it was the sight of a little blond girl playing beside a pond there that prompted him to conceive Dirk van der Heide and to imagine such an innocent sensorium reacting to the new sort of aerial mass murder. (Later, after the United States declared war, Young had the opportunity to experience such horror firsthand, as a uniformed war correspondent for the *Saturday Evening Post*.)

The very few intimates privy to Young's secret knew that he was donating the royalties from *My Sister and I* to Dutch War Relief. This will seem a puzzling gesture in light of the fact that it was less the Dutch than the British who were the propaganda beneficiaries of the book. In considering that anomaly, we must now notice another character entering this little drama. He is Frank Morley, one of Young's colleagues at Harcourt, Brace. The brother of the novelist and essayist Christopher Morley, Frank had been born in Baltimore but of British parents. He had attended New College, Oxford, as a Rhodes Scholar and married an Englishwoman. After working for Bruce Richmond on the *Times Literary Supplement*, he helped found the publishing firm of

Faber and Faber. He became so vividly Anglophile, in speech and dress and attitude, that sometimes it was hard to remember that he was an American. In the fall of 1939, significantly, he journeyed from London to New York to take up work as editor-in-chief at Harcourt, Brace, a house already well known as an important American outlet for the more impressive kinds of British writing, like the work of T. S. Eliot and I. A. Richards, Virginia Woolf and E. M. Forster. "Frank Morley," Mrs. Stanley Young remembers, "was extremely anxious to get America into the war against Hitler." I would propose that Morley returned to the States at this time specifically to assist the covert work of British propaganda in wearing down American neutrality. And I would propose further that his presence and mission were not unknown to the Canadian William Stephenson (the celebrated "Man Called Intrepid"), who managed the New York office of the bureau mock-innocently designated "British Security Co-ordination." Stephenson's office saw to it that the right articles got written, the right books got published, the right news items got planted, and the right speeches got delivered, all in aid of American intervention on Britain's side. And even more: Stephenson's operation produced flagrant forgeries arguing (largely fictitious) German designs on the Western Hemisphere. One of the masterpieces of his forgery studio was a bogus map of Latin America said to have been captured from the Germans. This showed Hitler's alleged plan for cutting up South and Central America into new Nazi states. So shrewdly made and cunningly disclosed was this item that President Roosevelt fell for it and delivered on October 27, 1941, a sincere radio speech, in which he said,

Hitler has often protested that his plans for conquest do not extend beyond the Atlantic Ocean. I have in my possession a secret map, made in Germany by Hitler's government—by planners of the new world order. It is a map of South America and Central America as Hitler proposes to organize it. . . . The geographical experts of Berlin . . . have ruthlessly obliterated all the existing boundary lines and have divided South America into five vassal states. . . . And they have also arranged it that the territory of one of these new puppet states includes the Republic of Panama and our great life-line, the Panama Canal. This map makes clear the Nazi designs . . . against the United States itself.

This was a triumph for Stephenson, one of his most success-ful performances. But as usual he had to go to work cau-tiously, lest he be found violating the American Neutrality Act. And it was not just the law he had to be careful about. It was many Americans' suspicions of perfidious Albion, still widely regarded as one of the most rapacious and unregener-ate of colonial powers. During an American lecture tour in 1939, Anthony Eden found that "many Americans regarded all British information as tainted." It is now clear that Ste-phenson's operation was much more sly and extensive then anyone could have imagined at the time. As one British intelligence officer said later, "From New York, while the United States was at peace [and later while it was at war], Britain ran the most intricate integrated intelligence and secret-operations organization in history." Isaiah Berlin, in the British Embassy in Washington, was part of it. So were

such as Noël Coward and W. Somerset Maugham, as they
traveled about the United States lecturing on innocent cultural subjects but ceaselessly observing and reporting back
home on the temper of the populace. The British Library of
Information, one of Stephenson's New York fronts, issued
hundreds of overt propaganda items like pamphlets titled
War-time Britain, British Colonial Policy, and *India,* and devoted
much attention to even such apparent trivialities as the paper
bookmark printed in England and imported in July 1941,
which reads on one side,

BRITAIN
AND HER
ALLIES ARE
RESOLVED
ON THIS * *
that come
what may
the menace of
a world ruled
by force alone
shall be lifted
from the hearts
of men
by the strength
of those
who stand for
FREEDOM.

(Untangled, that rhetoric says that Britain is determined that the United States shall enter the war.) The other side depicts a row of manned heavy machine guns aimed at the right, or eastern side, of the photograph, from which direction the Germans propose to invade England. On this side, the band-wagon appeal:

> MEN OF BRITAIN
> Over the seas that are
> guarded by Britain's
> invincible navy, the
> sister countries of the
> British Commonwealth
> are marshalling great
> hosts to join the three
> million men of the British
> Army now training
> in free Britain. The
> time is coming when
> the British Empire
> and her Allies will
> strike the great
> counter-blow to aggression
> which will set the
> world free again.

But in addition to such overt emanations, behind the scenes the office of British Security Co-ordination was conducting a massive campaign of gray propaganda, and Stephenson doubtless watched with satisfaction as Harcourt, Brace published Jan Struther's *Mrs. Miniver* and the Museum of Modern Art mounted an exhibition "Britain at War," to the text of whose catalog contributed no less than the Faber & Faber and Harcourt, Brace authors T. S. Eliot and Herbert Read. (One caption beneath a double spread of photographs of firemen, nurses, soldiers, sailors, and pilots speaks of "the unfamiliar beauty of the British race.") In those days, one informant has declared, the atmosphere at Harcourt, Brace was that of "an unofficial pro-Allied propaganda organization." From Harcourt, Brace also in 1941 came items like *Letters from the Women of Britain,* edited by Jan Struther, as well as Allan A. Michie and Walter Graebner's *Their Finest Hour: First-Hand Narratives of the War in England.* It now seems clear how much of the American perception of embattled, heroic Britain was created specifically by the firm of Harcourt, Brace.

Although unable to pinpoint the exact source of the infection, classic Britain-despisers like Edmund Wilson were convinced, as Mary McCarthy recalls, that the British "were trying to trick us into intervention." In April 1941, Charles A. Lindbergh addressed a large anti-interventionist rally in New York. Afterward, he wrote in his journal that he sensed "considerable anti-British feeling" in the audience, "a feeling that we are being pushed into war regardless of how the people feel about it, and that England is largely responsible for the mess we are being dragged into." And a few days later he observed: "The pressure for war is high and mounting," encouraged by "the 'intellectuals' and the 'Anglophiles' and the British agents who are allowed free reign. . . ." *My*

Sister and I is only one illustration of how right Wilson and Lindbergh were.

But for the British, the issue was obviously desperate, way beyond the normal conventions of something like honest dealing. In 1941 American neutrality seemed a menace to Britain's survival almost as ominous as the German army lined up in invasion posture along the French coast. America had to be got into the war, at the cost of any kind of skulduggery. Churchill knew this well. But so did the rank and file. In June 1941, a British soldier in North Africa voiced the obvious when he wrote in his diary: "I cannot see how we are going to win this war without the participation of America." After all this, the irony of America's ultimate entry into the war is almost too good to be true. It was not the lavish expenditure of British cunning and subtlety and scholarship and rhetoric that brought America in, but the crude, stupid, merely physical contingency of Pearl Harbor.

Now I'd like to leave the circumstances which produced *My Sister and I* and return to the character of its young protagonist and testifier. Dirk is conspicuous for his innocence, which operates in tandem with a very sharp intelligence. Despite his Dutch costuming, he is an ideal American character, allied at least by his courage, honesty, and decency to that great American original Huckleberry Finn—especially the sensitive Huck who looks on in helpless horror as murder is committed and people are savaged and humiliated. Dirk is an early wartime avatar of such similar innocent young creatures of the Second World War as William Saroyan's Homer Macauley, the sympathetic telegraph-delivery boy in his novel of 1943, *The Human Comedy.* But in an even more visible way, the innocent and intelligent Dirk foreshadows Holden Caulfield in J. D. Salinger's immensely popular *Catcher in the Rye,* a work which is more of a wartime performance than perhaps we remember. Part of it appeared first in 1945, as a short story in *Collier's;* more appeared in 1946, as a short story in *The New Yorker.* The whole was published in the summer of 1951. Placed next to *My Sister and I, The Catcher in the Rye* will seem notably "wartime." Holden Caulfield's innocence, intelligence, and integrity are close to Dirk's, although his enemies are not invading German troops but various types of "phonies" lurking in Pennsylvania and New York. Like Dirk, Holden is a version of Mrs. Deventer's "bewildered child in wartime," baffled by the ubiquity and impudence of evil. If Dirk's contact with apparently motiveless malignity, like the strafing of the civilians on the road, leads to puzzlement and anger, Holden's leads to a nervous breakdown—to his more intellectually sensitive understanding, the so-called rational world has revealed itself so little able to live up to its pretensions. "I can't sleep or write anymore now or anything": Dirk or Holden speaking? Hard to tell. And Dirk's pride in his sister Keetje and his solicitude for her innocence is like Holden's feeling for his little sister Phoebe. He would like to clean up all the lewd graffiti in the world so she will never see them.

Why does *My Sister and I* seem such an instructive example of writing in wartime? By presenting it as exemplary, am I suggesting that fraud or disingenuousness are the main characteristics of such writing, that, for example, Eliot's *Four*

Quartets was undertaken at the urging of the British Ministry of Information in order to make British spiritual life look good? Am I suggesting that Anne Frank never existed, or that some cunning, cynical artificer forged her diary? Not at all, although I would suggest that no one ever underestimate the likelihood that a given literary work published during the war was produced because someone in the information— that is, propaganda—services wanted it to be. But *My Sister and I* is typical of wartime writing in many ways. The benignity of Dirk and those he happens among can't help calling to mind the sentimentality and emotional primitivism and moral simplification among American wartime writers like Thornton Wilder, John Steinbeck, John Hersey, Archibald MacLeish, and Norman Corwin; and in England, J. B. Priestley and H. E. Bates. The OWI generation, they have been called, and most of their wartime writing (try, for example, to read Steinbeck's *The Moon Is Down* today) is virtually indistinguishable from the emissions of the Office of War Information. And sometimes the damage wrought by the wartime softening of the analytical faculties is not just thematic and doctrinal. It is syntactical and writerly as well. Consider the case of Carl Sandburg, who brought out in 1943 a collection of his flaccid, highminded wartime pieces titled *Home Front Memo*. Now no writer isolates and thus emphasizes on his first page a formal dedication without considerable thought and attention. Here is Sandburg's dedication:

This collection of pamphlets, speeches, broadcasts, newspaper columns, poems, legends, photograph texts, now

assembled and made available in one carry-all volume—
this is

Dedicated

to the life, works, and memory of

STEPHEN VINCENT BENÉT

who knew the distinction between pure art and propaganda in the written or spoken word. He could sing to
give men music, consolation, pleasure. He could intone
chant or prayer pointing the need for men to act. He
illustrated the code and creed of those writers who seek
to widen the areas of freedom for all men. . . . He saw
that a writer's silence on living issues can in itself constitute a propaganda of conduct leading toward the deteri-
oration or death of freedom. He wrote often hoping that
men would act because of his words. He could have been
Olympian, whimsical, seeking to be timeless amid bells
of doom not to be put off.

Nobody ever said Sandburg was a careful, or even a good
writer. But in that dedication, so seriously conceived, so
carefully designed to be portentous and effective, the war
has clearly solicited Sandburg's very worst—diction both
pretentious and sloppy, loose syntax, ineffective idiomatic
control ("pointing the need for"), vague figurative reali-
zation ("a propaganda of conduct"), and sheer rhetorical
stupidity ("He wrote often hoping that men would act because of his words"—a perfect way to praise Josef Goeb-
bels). Finally, stylistic pretentiousness collapsing into entire
disaster: *putting off bells of doom,* etc. It's true that it's easy
enough to ridicule writing like that. The point is not that

it is bad. The point is that in wartime it was taken to be not just good, but wonderful, and what we were fighting for. Only a few rowdies and subversives allowed themselves to say that it stank. Partly because the OWI generation enlisted literature in the cause of Victory—one used language like that at the time—the Allies won the war. But literature lost. It lost wit, nuance, moral outrage, irony, and contempt for philistinism and cant, and it replaced them with simple optimistic moral allegory of a kind fashionable even well after the war was over: consider James Gould Cozzens, Herman Wouk, and even Saul Bellow. It was the domination of the postwar perceptual scene by these and writers like them that finally triggered in reply the rowdy, contemptuous rejoinders of Kurt Vonnegut, Joseph Heller, and Thomas Pynchon, signaling that it was time for irony again.

Something similar is to be seen in the literary interpretation and criticism of the wartime period. It was not until after the war that it became appropriate to notice of Walt Whitman that he was not the humorless national gasbag, the tedious prophet and seer, which criticism had considered him for decades, but rather that he was a sly, furtive, disingenuous, deeply sensitive, private, and wonderfully devious artist. Less a declaimer than a meditator. Less a silly, diffuse enunciator of cosmic truths than a most subtle lyricist, teasing away at the very center of private being and perception.

The wartime Whitman, on the other hand, is the one presented in Gay Wilson Allen's *Walt Whitman Handbook* of 1946. Here Whitman is visited with impressive "ideas" and "positions": we hear much of his Pantheism and his Pan-psychism, his Transcendentalism and his Social Thought. We hear nothing of his subversiveness, his irony, his elusive dou-bleness, his uninnocent complexity and wit. Only in the 1950s, the war safely behind us, did we consent to receive a new Whitman, the one disclosed by such critics as Randall Jarrell, Richard Chase, and Leslie Fiedler. During the war, the old innocent Whitman had sufficed, and there was no motive to look for any other.

If for years you fancy that you are engaged in fighting utter evil, if every element and impulse of society is busy eradicat-ing wickedness, before long you will come to believe that therefore you yourself must incarnate pure goodness. As a result, there is sadly missing from most wartime writing the sense registered in C. Day Lewis's poem "Where Are the War Poets?" that fighting for our side against the Axis in-volves defending something pretty defective against some-thing even more loathsome. But during the war few cared to perceive that the battle was less between good and evil than between degrees of offensiveness. Everyone was obliged, in Day Lewis's words, to

Defend the bad against the worse.

Dwight Macdonald's understanding of this point, crucial to any sort of grown-up wartime intellectual life, prompted him to notice what a terrible person General George S. Patton was, what a menace to culture and mind, with his contempt for Jews and labor unions and (as he put it) "pacafism," and his enthusiasm for quasi-Nazi eugenics. Macdonald went so far as to say: "Far from the justness of the war excusing Patton's barbarism, Patton's barbarism calls into question the justness of the war."

The wartime atmosphere in which a Dirk van der Heide —and his fairy-tale wonderful British acquaintances—could seem believable is not easy to imagine now. It was a pre-Holocaust world, where Lin Yutang was valued as an ethical thinker and H. G. Wells as a prophet and Pearl Buck was taken to be an impressive novelist. The wartime instinct for moral purity helped to sustain Frank Buchman's Oxford Group and Moral Re-Armament movements. Clearly a Dirk van der Heide had to be invented, and one can appreciate the necessity of such a popular emblem of innocence by recalling that the normally sensitive and occasionally skeptical Alfred Kazin could forget himself in order to serve his country—in the pages of *The New Republic,* where he declared of Saroyan's *The Human Comedy* that its adolescent hero Homer Macauley "stands for the easy Saroyan knowledge of America . . . He stands for the struggle between his native innocence and the world's experience; and that is the point of [Saroyan's] story. This boy unites the American strands in himself; he carries them all. In his life can be heard the pulsing of all the telegraph keys over America. . . . All the locked doors open to this boy; all the reverberations of the national experience are to be heard in him." Too many *alls* there, surely. Kazin's point, acceptable, perhaps, as a wartime gesture, won't do at any other time—that is, if wit, profound knowledge, and deep adult understanding of evil and irony and tragedy are conceived as indispensable elements of "the national experience."

Finally, a historiographical note. If the data prove not to be what they are mistaken for, what hope for the more credulous sorts of historiography? In the large library I have been using, *My Sister and I,* cataloged of course under the name of the author *van der Heide, Dirk,* is to be found in the stacks not among the novellas but lodged with the memoirs and historical accounts, both informal and official, of life in the Low Countries during the Second World War. And pages of Stanley Young's book are invoked as an undoubted eyewitness account in Desmond Flower and James Reeves's anthology of war documents, *The Taste of Courage: The War, 1939–1945,* published in 1960. They begin their selection from *My Sister and I* with Dirk's innocent, boyish words, "Something terrible happened last night. War began!!!" Desmond Flower and James Reeves are proud that they have restricted their materials to, as they say, "documentary sources"; and their book jacket proclaims that here the reader will find "the words of those who took part in . . . the greatest war in history." Their selections, say the editors, document "how it actually felt to be alive [during the war]; to see, to hear, to smell, to feel the war at first hand"; and their selections are said to convey this intimacy specifically because they have been written by eyewitnesses and participants. Where the editors have had to call upon fiction, they have done so, they explain, only when they have been "satisfied that the writer was present at and witnessed the events. . . ."

It is all a testimony to the literary talent of Mr. Stanley Preston Young, who sensed both what the age and the United Kingdom demanded, and who supplied it in a memorable American way.

GEORGE ORWELL:
THE
CRITIC AS
HONEST MAN

Doubtless many theatergoers imagine that one of T. S. Eliot's most characteristic and important works is *Old Possum's Book of Practical Cats*, just as numerous TV-watchers must conceive that *Brideshead Revisited* represents Evelyn Waugh's talent at its most distinguished. Certainly middlebrow consensus has long celebrated *The Old Man and the Sea* as Hemingway's greatest achievement. A similar fate has fallen upon Orwell. His two works most vociferously celebrated are *Nine-*

teen Eighty-Four and *Animal Farm,* despite their demonstrating precisely his lack of great talent for either science-romance narrative or animal fable. In both, his anxiety that the essayistic message get across regardless occasions frequent narrative stoppage, overall clumsiness, and even something like archness. And indeed, the parts of *Nineteen Eighty-Four* one remembers with admiration are not narrative but strictly expository—the descriptions of the government and customs of Oceania, for example, or the mock-philological Appendix on "The Principles of Newspeak." Orwell is by nature an essayist, and even in his more engaging novels, like *Keep the Aspidistra Flying* and *Coming Up for Air,* essays keep breaking in.

An essayist obsessed with values: that's a fair working definition of a critic in general, and it's a good description of Orwell in particular. Although not immense, his critical output is large and impressive, and the kind of writers he has chosen to work on suggests at once his critical leanings. He's drawn to satirists and malcontents, like Swift and Smollett, and to "manly" novelists, writers like Kipling and Gissing, Conrad and Charles Reade and H. G. Wells. No one could tax Henry Miller with effeminacy, and Orwell's enthusiasm for the rude demotics of *The Tropic of Cancer* constitutes one of the most persuasive tributes Miller has ever received. Orwell's frequent adversions to Lawrence and Joyce suggest his susceptibility to the solid and downright, the "daily," as well as the soundness of his taste for contemporary work. The list of authors in whom he shows little interest is as significant: he dilates on no Romantic poets, no Renaissance writers except Shakespeare, no Henry James or Virginia

Woolf. Almost no Americans except Mark Twain. No Gide, no Proust, no Mann. A little bit of Russian novel, but not much. Little contemporary poetry except Yeats (Fascist tendencies noted) and Eliot (a great poet: too bad his piety makes him so silly). It's impossible to imagine him being interested in Wallace Stevens. He notices no literary theorists, philosophers, or aestheticians. In addition to essays on single authors, he performs numerous workouts in literary sociology, like the considerations of boys' weeklies and lewd seaside postcards and bookshop culture; and the treatments of the pamphlet as a genre and of Good Bad Books, of the psychology of the reviewer, and the respective attractiveness of books vs. cigarettes as things to spend money on. And preeminently, the essay "Politics and the English Language," which, widely anthologized, is now as familiar to hundreds of thousands of American college students as James Harvey Robinson's "Four Kinds of Thinking" used to be.

One can learn a lot about a critic by inferring his favorite substantive of disapprobation. For example, Ben Jonson's might be *indecorum*. Dryden's, *dullness*. Samuel Johnson's, *unnaturalness*. Wordsworth's, *artifice*. Coleridge's, *incoherence*. Arnold's, *provincialism*. Eliot's, *romanticism*. There's no doubt about Orwell's, for he uses it frequently and forcefully: it is *humbug*. For all its weaknesses, he loves *Tropic of Cancer* because he detects no humbug in it, another way of saying that Miller registers without affectation "everyday facts and everyday emotions." Literary pomposity and mental dishonesty are Orwell's constant targets, and his aim is sharp partly because he knows the book business so well. It is not every critic who has had the advantage of working in a bookshop and seeing at firsthand the wide difference between what people praise and what they read. Orwell's street-smart instinct for the facts of books recalls Johnson's, and there are numerous Orwellisms fit to be compared with Johnson's observation, "People seldom read a book which is given to them." Satirizing one Martin Walter, a commercial "teacher of writing" who has claimed that his formulas for "plotting" have produced many successful writers, Orwell asks, "Who are these successful writers whom Mr. Walter has launched upon the world? Let us hear their names, and the names of their published works, and then we shall know where we are." The tone is that of Johnson asking James Macpherson to produce the Ossianic manuscripts, as well as that of Johnson observing of Macpherson, said to have argued that there is no difference between virtue and vice, "If he does really think that there is no distinction between virtue and vice, why, Sir, when he leaves our houses, let us count our spoons." Orwell's nose for literary pretentiousness and cant is as acute as Johnson's sniffing out Thomas Gray's bogus classicism. "For anyone who wants a good laugh," Orwell writes, "I recommend . . . I. A. Richards's *Practical Criticism,*" that classic exposé of the pretentiousness and incapacity of a selection of Cambridge students of literature. Orwell did not attend a university.

Immersed in the book trade, observing all day behavior in the bookshop and the rental library, Orwell grows naturally into a skeptical and empirical critic. Confronting the great piles of remainders, he can't help noticing the ultimate fate of books pronounced, on their first appearance, masterpieces. He sees that their pages serve finally as food for worms, their dusty tops the graves of bluebottles. As he says in "Confessions of a Book Reviewer," "It is almost impossible to mention books in bulk without grossly overpraising the great majority of them. Until one has some kind of professional relationship with books one does not discover how bad the majority of them are." Nor does one learn other things that a good critic must know, like the frequency with which the title of an essay or book is the creation of an editor, not the author, and even that elements of the author's text are often the result of an editor's insisting that you can't *say* that. As if he ate and slept with *A Tale of a Tub* by his side, Orwell shares Swift's vision of the relation of literature to the book trade, and he perceives in a very eighteenth-century way that although literature is many other things as well, one thing it surely is, is a social institution, that every act of reading is an implicit social transaction. Thus he likes to speculate about the social causes and contexts of literary phenomena, "the *external* conditions that make certain writers popular at certain times." Why, for example, was Housman all the rage in the teens and twenties? For one thing, he could be regarded as a "country" poet, purveying a form of nostalgic compensation to newly urbanized readers of the "*rentier*-professional class," as well as gratifying their snobbery about "belonging to the country and despising the town." Fake-civilized people, Orwell notes, "enjoy reading about rustics (key phrase, 'close to the soil') because they imagine them to be more primitive and passionate than themselves." The collapse of religion also lies behind the vogue of Housman, who was seen to be "satisfyingly anti-Christian." A few years later, after the Great War, anthropological pessimism came in (like plus fours). One read Spengler and went Abroad. Money was easy, and "Everyone with a safe £500 a year turned highbrow and began training himself in *tædium vitae*." And so it goes. Literature is less the result of inexplicable subjective impulse than of compensatory social urges. Instructed by honest observation, Orwell learns in the bookshop about "the rarity of really bookish people," the frequency with which Austen and Thackeray are toted home from the shop but never opened. The opening chapter of *Keep the Aspidistra Flying,* depicting young Gordon Comstock's ennui and disdain working in Mr. McKechnie's bookshop and rental library, is probably as good a guide as any to the essence of Orwell's critical understanding and method. "If we did get a writer worth reading, should we know him when we saw him, so choked as we are with trash?" He is fascinated by the pathology of literary bad taste and loves to display ironically the names of novelists (Ethel M. Dell, Hugh Walpole, Warwick Deeping) once thought as attractive as Herman Wouk, Leon Uris, and James A. Michener.

[Orwell can remind us of how useful a guide to the current literary and educational situation attention to bookshop practices might be. The scheme of classification in chain book outlets will tell posterity the whole depressing news about current taste. The sign "Literature" designates the section containing fairly good novels (only). "Fiction" means bad novels, "Romance" bad novels for female readers. "Biography" means ghost-written memoirs of the shabby-famous. "Travel" means guidebooks, never travel books. "Occult" means books for adolescents. "Nonfiction" is divided into "Health" (sex and pornography) and "Self-improvement" (jogging and dieting). The section formerly labeled "Essays" or "Belles Lettres" or "Criticism" has simply disappeared. *Nineteen Eighty-Four* and *Animal Farm* will be found under Literature, but *Down and Out in Paris and London, The Road to Wigan Pier,* and *Homage to Catalonia* will not be in the shop at all. There's no classification for them.]

When in "England Your England" Orwell specifies as characteristic of the English "the lack of philosophical faculty, the absence . . . of any need for an ordered system of thought or even for the use of logic," he comes close to autobiographical description. A vigorous independence of mind, a freedom from all critical theory and "schools," is Orwell's hallmark. He can't even be designated a Socialist critic, because his Socialism is constantly succumbing to an aristocratic awareness that quality and freedom matter terribly. In his essay "The Prevention of Literature" he sketches a description of the traditional good writer as necessarily a heretic: formerly, he says, "His outlook was summed up in the words of the Revivalist hymn:

Dare to be a Daniel,
Dare to stand alone;
Dare to have a purpose firm,
Dare to make it known."

"To bring this hymn up to date," he adds, "one would have to add a 'Don't' at the beginning of each line." For all Orwell's distance from conventional religion, his is the spirit of British Dissent, and when he is playing Daniel it is difficult not to think of Bunyan, Milton, or Blake. This is why there's no critic like him.

He is certainly in what he recognizes as "the Liberal tradition," but if he rather resembles Edmund Wilson in the breadth of his curiosity and the firmness of his principles, his is a much more political imagination—Wilson seems hardly to have recognized that the Second World War was taking place. And if he has quite a lot in common with Lionel Trilling, with whom he shares a similar social-moral sense, his impulses are more activist. "No one can embrace Orwell's works," says E. M. Forster, "who hopes for ease," and no one can go to his criticism with any hope of extracting a formula, dialectic, or method. For those now weary of the successive orthodoxies of neo-Marxism, structuralism, and deconstruction, he is a distinct relief. His only tools are sensitivity and intelligence, and they inform him that books are written by human beings who hope to make a "statement" about something, that "propaganda in some form or other lurks in every book," that "our aesthetic judgments are always colored by our prejudices and beliefs." Orwell knows that even poems are, willy-nilly, about something: that's why they stop when they've finished being about what they're about. His legacy to succeeding critics can be summed up in a word: sense. His awareness of the irrational element in humanity, in politics, and in writing and art keeps him from imposing rationalistic expectations that invite the erection of a structure of critical assumptions. In "Wells, Hitler, and the World State" he accurately locates H. G. Wells's defect: he can't conceive how people can be so irrational as to follow

Hitler. "Wells is too sane," Orwell concludes, "to understand the modern world."

Just as he often echoes Johnson in tone and texture, so in his general critical approach. When Voltaire denigrated Shakespeare for his inattention to the classical unities and for the mess and irrationality of his works, Johnson defended him vigorously and Britishly: literature is what works empirically, not what assumes proper shapes. Likewise Orwell defends Shakespeare on the same grounds from the attacks of Tolstoy, who demands of a great author some highminded view, philosophical or religious, of life in general, together with a nearer approach than Shakespeare shows to an orderly, systematic, sensible technique. Tolstoy demands in an author, Orwell says, "dignity of subject-matter, sincerity, and good craftsmanship. . . . As Shakespeare is debased in outlook, slipshod in execution and incapable of being sincere even for a moment, he obviously stands condemned." But now Orwell brings up "a difficult question": "If Shakespeare is all that Tolstoy has shown him to be, how did he ever come to be so generally admired?" Orwell's answer, like Johnson's, is to invoke the irrational but human nature of the common reader. "There is no argument by which one can defend a poem. It defends itself by surviving, or it is indefensible." On that firm skeptical hook Orwell, quintessential British empiricist as he is, hangs all his criticism.

Because one's critical operations are not rational, one can honestly take pleasure in writings one knows to be artistically defective. "Art is not the same thing as cerebration," Orwell observes in his little essay on "Good Bad Books." "One can be amused or excited or moved by a book that one's intellect simply refuses to take seriously." For Orwell, critical systems are a totalitarianism, a menace in literature as in life. While wondering how a second-rater like H. G. Wells achieved such a powerful hold on the young of his generation, Orwell drops in a significant *systematically:*

> Back in the nineteen-hundreds it was a wonderful experience for a boy to discover H. G. Wells. There you were, in a world of pedants, clergymen, and golfers, with your future employers exhorting you to "get on or get out," your parents *systematically* warping your sexual life, and your dull-witted schoolmasters sniggering over their Latin tags; and here was this wonderful man . . . who *knew* that the future was not going to be what respectable people imagined.

The *ad hoc* is thus always preferable to any system. Orwell's loyalty to the empirical in part reflects his almost neurotic sensitivity to physical reality. His critical sensibility is nourished by the details of life—chairs and tables, coins, type sizes, printed ephemera, ordinary people. "Not uninteresting" is a phrase that recurs. His behavior illustrates Terence's *Homo sum; humani nil a me alienum puto.* "For casual reading— in your bath, for instance, or late at night when you are too tired to go to bed, or in the odd quarter of an hour before lunch—there is nothing to touch a back number of the *Girl's Own Paper.*" For him, the trouble with literary people, theoretical critics, and the "left intelligentsia" is "emotional shallowness": they "live in a world of ideas and have little contact with physical reality." When the reference book *Twentieth Century Authors* solicited an autobiographical note, he declared that his business was to "write books and raise hens and vegetables." Indeed, "Outside my work the thing I care most about is gardening, especially vegetable gardening." What other literary critic would include, as part of his career, experience as a tramp and a resident of "Common Lodging Houses"? Of what other critic writing in the early forties could it be said, as Frederic Warburg, his editor and publisher, has said of Orwell, "He was . . . a very keen Home Guard sergeant"? We can begin to infer some critical obligations identifiable as Orwellian:

1. The critic should read everything all the time— labels, signs, pamphlets, corporate reports, college catalogs, poems, novels, plays, "non-fiction," press releases—the lot. His business is language and its behavior in relation to human beings and their desires. The critic should beware generic snobbery—literature has its social classes just like life.

2. He should go in fear of any orthodoxy, political, religious, nationalistic, or literary.

3. Skeptical of orthodoxies, the critic should exercise his sense of humor and proportion and develop his capacity to take pleasure, sheer pleasure, in reading and writing.

4. He should be interested in everything: the love life of toads, the way tortoises drink and the poor die, the dynamics of anti-Semitism, the differences between Caslon and sans-serif types, the motives impelling ordinary people to read, why books get written at all, the price of food, the reason women do not as a rule become stamp collectors, and the reason shipwrecks and trial scenes are literary staples.

The critic should be able, like Orwell, to get an idea of the riches of the New World by noting of Mark Twain's America that the smallest coin then circulating was equivalent not to a British penny but a British shilling.

5. In his critical writing he should strive for absolute honesty, even at the cost of occasional personal humiliation. "To see what is in front of one's nose needs a constant struggle," he says, and he knows that many of one's youthful enthusiasms would sorely embarrass the mature critic. As Orwell puts it: "I think that any critic . . . must have many passages in his youth that he would willingly keep dark." (How often do we hear from a critic that at one time he greatly admired e e cummings or Somerset Maugham?) "Lies" really bother him, and Gordon Comstock's indictment of advertising as nothing but lying is heartfelt Orwell, a foretaste of his later outraged assault on the language of political duplicity. The main thing he admires in Smollett is his "outstanding intellectual honesty." He exhorts intellectuals to look into themselves without equivocation for traces of anti-Semitism, having noticed that the writer deploring it most often "fails to start his investigation in the one place where he could get hold of some reliable evidence—that is, in his own mind."

Anatomized this way, Orwell might seem merely bluff and simpleminded, strong, to be sure, but wanting in subtlety and artistic guile. But actually he is a master of the kind of critical discourse that turns on itself, that plays with the reader, establishing a tactical dynamics of ambiguity, surprise, dualism, even fruitful contradiction. For example: in the early part of his essay on Dickens, he seems to invite us to patronize Dickens as something close to "a reactionary humbug" who counts on "a change of heart" to ameliorate the human condition. And the reader comfortably settles into this position. But actually, Orwell goes on, looked at from a slightly different angle, Dickens appears a thoroughgoing hater of tyranny and thus a genuine, though "moral," revolutionary: "It is not at all certain that a merely moral criticism of society may not be just as 'revolutionary'—and revolution, after all, means turning things upside down—as the politico-economic criticism which is fashionable at this moment [1939]." In real life and in Dickens—and we can add in Orwell as well—"The moralist and the revolutionary are constantly undermining each other." Hence the necessity of ambiguity and complication.

Orwell performs a similar operation in his essay on Kipling. First, he attacks him with all the usual charges: he is undeniably a sadist, a "pre-Fascist," an imperialist. But the "turn" to a less moralistic, self-righteous view of Kipling operates as an invitation to the reader to peer into himself:

> We all live by robbing Asiatic coolies, and those of us who are "enlightened" all maintain that those coolies ought to be set free; but our standard of living, and hence our "enlightenment," demands that the robbery shall continue.

And as Orwell proceeds, he turns Kipling around until the reader is obliged to see another side: Kipling the hater of war and the writer of some of the best good bad poetry in

English, from which no one but "a snob and a liar" could deny receiving pleasure. Kipling had "a certain grip on reality," and it was not his fault that reality was what it was. If it is true that he identified himself with a fatuous ruling class, "he gained a corresponding advantage from having at least tried to imagine what action and responsibility are like." Furthermore, "It is a great thing in his favor that he is not witty, not 'daring,' has no wish to *épater les bourgeois.*" Conducted through these twists and turns of balancing and weighing, the reader has been brought to discrimination. He is finally asked to confront this critical paradox and to make of it what he may: "Kipling deals in thoughts which are both vulgar and permanent." Like Shakespeare, but of course not as good. Here as everywhere, dogmatic, monolithic certainty is the critical enemy. Is it a good thing to be, like Henry Miller, inside the whale, protected by one's "art" from noticing the larger troubles of the outside world? Well, yes, in one way, any appearance at all of "the autonomous individual" being a refreshing sight in a world of totalitarians and zombies. In another way, of course, not at all. In fact, quite irresponsible. And yet—

Such complicated unwillingness to decide absolutely finds a corollary in one of Orwell's most notable stylistic techniques. He will often combine two quite contradictory rhetorical gestures, one, as it were, giving, the other taking away. On the one hand, an enactment of total sincerity, as in the *earnestly* in "I earnestly counsel anyone who has not done so to read . . . *Tropic of Cancer.*" Or sometimes recourse to the "sincere" second-person address: "You never walk far through any poor quarter of any big town without coming upon a small newsagent's shop." Or, after quoting an apparently odd utterance by Cyril Connolly: "When you read the second sentence in this passage, your natural impulse is to look for the misprint." But on the other hand, while such gestures of intimate honesty are going on, an equal but opposite movement will begin to take place: obvious exaggeration and overstatement and even "lying," as in the *never* and the *anys* in the sentence about the newsagent's shop. One passage in "Inside the Whale" very clearly exemplifies this characteristic double movement. It begins with what appears to be honest confession, motivated by a sincere desire to be accurate and fair, an opponent of exaggeration:

> Some years ago I described Auden as "a sort of gutless Kipling." As criticism this was quite unworthy, indeed it was merely a spiteful remark, but it is a fact that in Auden's work, especially his earlier work, an atmosphere of uplift—something rather like Kipling's *If* or Newbolt's *Play up, Play up and Play the Game!*—never seems to be very far away.

Thus far honest discrimination. Now for the opposite, the irresponsible, misleading exaggeration, pivoting on words like *pure* and *exact*.

> Take, for instance, a poem like "You're leaving now, and it's up to you boys." It is pure scout-master, the exact

note of the ten-minutes' straight talk on the dangers of self-abuse.

The effect is of course comic, and one impression given off is that criticism is an activity too human for solemnity. Or inappropriate exactitude.

Such a glance at Orwell's verbal technique may prompt the question, How well should a critic write? F. R. Leavis, says Lachlan Mackinnon, "was doggedly determined not to write well," and one hardly goes to Kenneth Burke, William Empson, W. K. Wimsatt, or the later R. P. Blackmur for the pleasures of their prose. Orwell, on the other hand, asserts in "Why I Write" that writing an essay would be insupportable if it were not, in addition to an intellectual, "also an esthetic experience." "I shall continue," he says, "to feel strongly about prose style," and his feeling strongly about it makes his prose the clearest and least pompous in modern criticism. As he sees it, there are two moral defects which issue in bad writing: one is laziness, the other pretentiousness. He implies an immunity to both when, in "Politics and the English Language," he comes out with the phrase "the work of prose-construction" to suggest what it takes to write well and goes on to list the techniques by which such hard work is "habitually dodged": dying metaphors, jargony verbs ("render inoperative"), passive voice, meaningless words, needless multiplication of syllables ("the fact that"). So flagrant are these techniques not just in political rhetoric but in art and literary criticism, he finds, that "it is normal to come across long passages which are almost completely lacking in meaning." For Orwell, one contributor of meaninglessness is the popularity among critics of terms which are mere emotional triggers. *Sentimental* was one in his day. "I once began making a list of writers whom the critics called 'sentimental.' In the end it included nearly every English writer. The word is in fact a meaningless symbol of hatred. . . ." Today he might zero in on *reductive,* or *simplistic,* or *authentic,* terms as offensive as *beautiful* in Orwell's day. The cause of bad writing, especially of criticism, is specifically "literary society." Things might improve, he suggests, if novels could be reviewed not by "reviewers" but by amateurs: "A man who is not a practiced writer but has just read a book which has deeply impressed him is more likely to tell you what it is *about* than a competent but bored professional."

Just as Pound (not one of Orwell's idols) was learning to write poems by the technique of excision, cutting everything not strictly necessary, Orwell was learning to do the same in prose. Rigorously jettisoning unnecessary words (usually prepositions or *gradus* modifiers) in order to let the meaning leap forth is one of his devices for achieving clarity, and at the same time suggesting a special sincerity and honesty. As he writes Roger Senhouse in 1948, "I may be wrong, but my instinct is simplicity every time." Thus he is proud to write *Coming Up for Air* without using a single semicolon, "an unnecessary stop." Warburg testifies that "nothing had to be done" with Orwell's copy. "Really nothing. Orwell as a writer was less trouble I should think than anybody I've ever met," which is to say that no one had to spend time cutting inert adjectives and removing padding from his sentences.

A critic's impulse to be simple and clear may be taken

as a sign of personal generosity, evidence of a hope that many
will be able to share his perceptions unimpeded. Orwell's
personal generosity was remarkable, and it was fearless. In
one of his London Letters to *Partisan Review* (Winter 1945)
he invited all readers of that magazine visiting London (they
would be American soldiers, largely) to look him up and talk
literature and politics. He reminds them that during working
hours he can be found at the offices of the *Tribune*. He then
adds: "But failing that my home number is CAN 3751." I
find that astonishing. Imagine any other well-known critic
risking boredom by inviting hundreds of earnest aspirants to
drop in anytime. If it's hard to imagine in 1945, it's harder
to imagine today. Alfred Kazin just might do that. So might
Irving Howe. Most American critics would not, including
specifically Edmund Wilson.

But "saints should always be judged guilty until they
are proved innocent," as Orwell says at the beginning of his
essay on Gandhi. Orwell certainly has his defects and limitations. For one thing, once he goes much further back than
the middle of the nineteenth century, his historical imagination fails him. He has trouble understanding a society which
is not Liberal. This is the main reason he's not satisfying on
Gulliver's Travels. While recognizing its context in "politics,"
he ignores its context in religious politics, missing, for example, the reason Swift satirizes the Dutch so vigorously—
they were famous for religious toleration, which to Swift
meant they were really crypto-atheists. As a religious skeptic
and socialist, Orwell is a sucker for the Houyhnhnms and
takes them as seriously as they do themselves. Skilled at some
kinds of satire himself, he doesn't always seem to understand

that satire is by nature negative and destructive, just as, say, pastoral is positive. It's Orwell's strong sense of justice that gets in the way. Humor fails him, for example, when he instances one of Swift's (or rather Gulliver's) wildly comic "lists" as evidence of Swift's "irresponsible violence." Gulliver asserts that his reconciliation with the Yahoo kind back in England

> might not be so difficult if they would be content with those vices and follies only which nature hath entitled them to. I am not in the least provoked at the sight of a lawyer, a pickpocket, a colonel, a fool, a lord, a gamester, a politician, a whoremonger, a physician, an evidence, a suborner, an attorney, a traitor, or the like.

Missing the point entirely, Orwell explains with weary, literal-minded patience: "The list lumps together those who break the conventional code, and those who keep it. For instance, if you automatically condemn a colonel, as such, on what grounds do you condemn a traitor? Or again, if you want to suppress pickpockets, you must have laws, which means that you must have lawyers." He concludes of Swift's performance here: "One has the feeling that personal animosity is at work." To which the only answer is, Yes. Orwell is too goodhearted to be trusted with eighteenth-century satire, and sometimes he talks as if the world always should have been modern, as if through some oversight it failed to be modern until the nineteenth century. In his essay on Dickens he seems disappointed that Dickens is not more like Jack London. And sometimes he allows his rage for justice to overcome his tact, as in his essay "Looking Back on the Spanish War." Most of it is written precisely in the rabble-rousing idiom ("the lords of property and their hired liars and bumsuckers") reprehended in "Politics and the English Language." And even in "politics" he sometimes exhibits astonishing blindness. For one thing, until the end of the war he can't conceive that the Germans are simply killing off the Jews. He is too nice to imagine that. As late as 1943 he understands that the vignette of "elderly Jewish professors flung into cesspools" conveys an image of extreme Nazi misbehavior and that adversion to "pogroms and deportations" virtually sums up the matter. What prevents his suspecting the worst is simply his insufficiently developed sense of evil. Wholly secular, he lacks an equivalent of the conception of original sin.

On the other hand, with contemporary writing he is wonderfully sound. Although he doubtless overrates Henry Miller—largely, one suspects, because he constitutes a stench in genteel nostrils—he knows that Lawrence and Joyce are good and that Sean O'Casey is not. He recognizes Eliot's distinction while condescending to his religion and despising his politics. He knows that the "modern" part of Quiller-Couch's *Oxford Book of English Verse* is a national disgrace. Acutely, he senses that something's the matter with Aldous Huxley, that his work will survive as little as Wells's. Orwell made as few mistakes as anyone in estimating the ultimate value of his contemporaries.

At this moment, as literary criticism grows daily more pretentious, more afflicted with delusions of power and authority, more "theory"-ridden and remote, Orwell is a refreshing counterweight, with his eye focused on such actual operative literature as Boys' Weeklies and seaside postcards. His example has doubtless encouraged a reawakened interest in the generic conventions of kinds of writing not normally in high repute as literature—travel books, memoirs, histories, and the like—as well as literary forms too daily and commonplace to be considered artistic, like letters to the editor and "personal," i.e., lonely hearts, classified ads. Their inevitable and touching element of self-praise ("Clever non-smoking intellectual man desires friendship with a woman who thinks and jogs") Orwell was entirely free of. He lived only forty-six years, and when tuberculosis killed him he died without self-pity or complaint, or even wonder. I think that, as well as his critical performance, sets a good example.

"A Power of
Facing
Unpleasant
Facts"

The words are Orwell's, in his essay "Why I Write." From childhood, he says, he might have sensed that he was going to be a writer, for already he had "a facility with words and a power of facing unpleasant facts." The latter, he implies throughout his career, is necessary not just to any writer but to any honest thinker. And it's notably a *power,* not merely a talent or a flair. The power of facing unpleasant facts is clearly an attribute of decent, sane grown-ups as opposed to the immature, the silly, the nutty, or the doctrinaire.

Some exemplary unpleasant facts are these: that life is short and almost always ends messily; that if you live in the actual world you can't have your own way; that if you do get what you want, it turns out not to be the thing you wanted; that no one thinks as well of you as you do yourself; and that one or two generations from now you will be forgotten entirely and that the world will go on as if you had never existed. Another is that to survive and prosper in this world you have to do so at someone else's expense or do and undergo things it's not pleasant to face: like, for example, purchasing your life at the cost of the innocents murdered in the aerial bombing of Europe and the final bombing of Hiroshima and Nagasaki. And not just the bombings. It's also an unpleasant fact that you are alive and well because you or your representatives killed someone with bullets, shells, bayonets, or knives, if not in Germany, Italy, or Japan, then Korea or Vietnam. You have connived at murder, and you thrive on it, and that fact is too unpleasant to face except rarely.

Orwell confronted a number of people unwilling to face their own kind of unpleasant facts. One was his first publisher, Victor Gollancz. During the 1930s Gollancz ran the Left Book Club, whose 40,000 members received regularly a work designed to sustain their liberal principles. He commissioned Orwell's *The Road to Wigan Pier* (1937), his famous study of depression poverty in the Midlands. But when Orwell's manuscript came in, it revealed a mighty unpleasant fact. The first half was highly acceptable, being fully in accord with the Left view of things. It depicted the horror of labor in the coal mines, the vicious conditions under which the miners lived, their terrible food and sordid housing and impossibility of escape. Clearly a strong case for socialism, and Gollancz was pleased with that. It was the second half of Orwell's manuscript that was the shocker, for there Orwell exposed the sentimental and self-delusive socialist notion of a classless society. He indicated how class-conscious he was himself and would always be, one unpleasant fact being that one never shakes off the class gestures and prejudices in which one has been nurtured. Orwell did argue that socialism might be a partial solution to social ills, but he noted extensively (and perhaps with a bit too much visible pleasure, the pleasure of the instinctive satirist) the objectionable personal attributes of socialists that kept the ordinary person from taking their doctrines seriously. Too many were sandal-wearers and health-food consumers, cranks, teetotalers, Marxist jargon-merchants. Orwell went so far as to say: "The fact is that Socialism, *in the form in which it is now presented,* appeals chiefly to unsatisfactory or even inhuman types." It's not hard to imagine Gollancz, together with the other two directors of the Left Book Club, John Strachey and Harold Laski, turning quite purple at that indictment. Nor did Gollancz like any better another of Orwell's perceptions, that "Socialism . . . smells of . . . machine-worship and the stupid cult of Russia," whose typical commissar he stigmatized as "half gangster, half gramophone."

So appalled was Gollancz by this that at first he tried to persuade Orwell to supply the Left Book Club with the first, innocent part of the book only, and to publish the rest, if he really had to say those offensive things, somewhere else.

But Orwell, the honest man, of course rejected this cop-out, and Gollancz's only recourse was to honor his contract and publish the whole embarrassing thing but to try to take some of the sting out by writing his own Foreword critical of Orwell's uncertain—that is, complex, ironic, and thus fully human—socialist vision. To do this he had to utter obvious lies, among them, "The Left Book Club has no 'policy.'" And the only means Gollancz can find to deal with Orwell's anti-Soviet position is *ad hominem* attack and a disgustingly irrelevant search for motives. He speaks of "Mr. Orwell's unresolved conflict"—between admiring the ideal of socialism while despising some of its actual results, as if that made him some kind of psychological freak. Gollancz goes on to point out that, Orwell being a writer, it is not hard "to understand why Mr. Orwell states that almost all people of real sensitiveness, and in particular almost all writers and artists and the like, are hostile to Socialism. . . ." The unpleasant fact Victor Gollancz has had to face is that he has hired a real person, not a toady or gramophone, to do a job of honest perception and expression. Gollancz, would-be censor and tyrant, clearly never thought of applying to himself Orwell's ringing assertion near the end of *The Road to Wigan Pier:* "Socialism means the overthrow of tyranny, at home as well as abroad."

Another example of anxiety in the face of unpleasant facts, this one considerably closer to home. *The Daily Pennsylvanian,* the independent student newspaper of the University of Pennsylvania, has distinguished itself by honoring in action the axiom of all respectable journalists: What someone doesn't want you to publish is journalism; all else is publicity. On Alumni Day, May 15, 1987, thousands of Penn alumni, including hundreds of graduates of the university's Wharton School (of business), assembled for old times' sake, as that day's *Daily Pennsylvanian* noted in one of its articles headlined "Alumni Return for Graduation Weekend; Record Gifts Expected." Regrettably, on the front page some unpleasant facts greeted the alumni: "Four Students Arrested for Dealing Drugs," for example, and "Report Names Senior [University] VP in Police Cover-up." But that day's really striking unpleasant fact was conveyed by a story in the most conspicuous place on the front page, the upper right-hand position: "Wharton Prof Charged with Raping Child." It sounded like something from the April Fool's Day edition, but alas, it wasn't. The story revealed that a forty-seven-year-old professor of accounting had been arrested, charged, and released on $10,000 bail for allegedly committing offenses against his four-year-old step-granddaughter, including rape, statutory rape, involuntary deviate sexual intercourse, indecent assault, and corruption of a minor. As usual, copies of *The Daily Pennsylvanian* were available in stacks around the campus.

From the reaction of certain professors and administrators of the Wharton School, the editors of *The Daily Pennsylvanian,* confident of the facts in this story, which have never been disputed, could infer with some pride that they were performing real journalism, not cover-up, publicity, or advertising. Apparently despairing of rebutting the unpleasant facts or asserting their falsity, as Victor Gollancz might have been tempted to do, authorities at the Wharton School simply began removing the newspapers so the well-heeled alumni wouldn't see them. In all, about 1,000 copies of the offending paper were hustled out of sight, and one unfortunate Associate Professor of Marketing was photographed (by the alert *Daily Pennsylvanian*) carrying away a bundle of the papers to hide or destroy them.

And this was not the first time unpleasant facts had been deemed too ripe for the university's clientele. A year earlier, a stack of the newspapers had been removed from a university building frequented by prospective students and their parents when employees of the admissions office found themselves appalled by a front-page article about a stabbing on the campus.

If the attempt to conceal unpleasant facts on these two occasions was unseemly, not just at a university devoted to the free play of the mind over all subjects but anywhere the First Amendment might be conceived as a guide to civilized behavior, worse was the statement of justification issued by the Office of the Dean of the Wharton School once the Alumni Day scandal had been exposed:

The Wharton School confirms that on Friday, May 15, copies of the *Daily Pennsylvanian* were removed from two buildings at the school, and it is regrettable that this has caused concern within the University community. . . .

The Wharton School strongly believes in freedom of speech and of the press, but it also believes in news reporting that reflects all facets—the positive as well as the negative—of the University. Friday's edition of the *Daily Pennsylvanian,* which focussed on allegations of rape,

drug use and administrative cover-ups, was most inappropriate and not balanced reporting when 3,500 alumni
were returning to their alma mater. Many who saw the
front page felt that the overall negative impression conveyed to alumni was not reflective of the current state of
a great University that has much to be proud of.

Anyone interested in the ethics of rhetoric would want to
spend some time contemplating the more swinish elements
of that statement: the evasive passive voice (*copies . . . were
removed*) and pompous waffle (*it is regrettable*) cunningly avoid-
ing mention of the agents of action so that no one will be
moved to ask, "Who, precisely, was responsible?"; the notion
that some facts are *most inappropriate* because they are unpleasant, despite their being uttered in a setting devoted to
little more than freedom of inquiry and the development of
bold intellect; the phrase *balanced reporting,* designed to conceal the meaning, *reporting I like because it makes me and my fief
look good;* the near-candid admission that what hurt was the
effect of the facts on the alumni's willingness to part with
large amounts of money; and finally, the assumption that the
function of news reporting is to publicize "the current state
of a great university" rather than to deliver accurate data,
regardless of its ultimate use or implications. In addition,
how could the newspaper in this case perform "news reporting" reflecting positive, as well as negative "facets"? It certainly tried. It tried to give the accused professor a chance to
reveal the silver lining in his indictment, but when phoned
he refused to indicate a positive side—indeed, to comment
at all on the charges. Nor did his lawyer consent to suggest

a positive side. What was the paper to do but to go with what it had? Even the Wharton School statement does not say that the unpleasant facts are untrue; merely that they are "inappropriate." That word appears also in an apology issued by the luckless associate professor photographed toting away the bundles of papers. He is finally obliged to acknowledge that "the paper has the right to publish whatever it wants, regardless of how inappropriate I believe the paper to be in its editorial judgment regarding timing, content, and placement."

The attempt in these documents to equate *appropriateness* or *balance* or *fairness* with a view of things held by oneself will sound familiar to those who recall Richard Nixon's neurotic inability to accept criticism, an external sign of much deeper defects. Noting unfavorable comments by the journalists Hugh Sidey and John Osborne, Nixon sent a memorandum to H. R. Haldeman in April 1972, ordering that in revenge the two offending reporters be denied White House privileges. Nixon concluded: "What we have to realize is the cold fact that both Sidey and Osborne are totally against us. They are not honest reporters." The perverse logical relation of the last two clauses will suggest sufficiently what's wrong with both Nixon's and the Wharton School's way of thought, although Nixon's may be considered the more forgivable because he was not a prominent officer of a university, merely a cheap pol engaged in his customary attempt to rescue his reputation from the scrutiny of the honest.

Because they were pursuing an end not dishonorable, the sprouts of *The Daily Pennsylvanian* were able to see the issue more clearly and responsibly than their elders. Later, the paper commented, with a pleasant lack of equivocation, "It is easier to suppress information than it is to cope with it. Proclaiming the virtues of free speech is a nice gesture, but respecting such principles requires character." And the student writer went on: "The *DP* is not in the business of putting a happy face on the news. . . . The implication [in the Wharton School's statement on the matter] that the newspaper should have held the stories until the alumni left patronizes them as well as compromising the purpose of the university." Well reasoned, sprout, and well written!

I have dealt with the actions of Victor Gollancz and the Wharton School and Richard Nixon because, although lots of time and space separates them, their behavior when faced with unpleasant facts and honest talk they don't like strikes me as so instructively typical of a modern moral insensitivity among otherwise quite sophisticated people. I have authors especially in mind, those authors who, not liking the reviews their books receive, feel obliged to insist publicly that the comment of the reviewer is, variously, unfair, perverse, stupid, irresponsible, or otherwise not at all what it should be —that is, laudatory.

I have descanted on this subject before, in an essay called "Being Reviewed," and indeed the topic has been a favorite ever since encountering Samuel Johnson's classic observation, in his *Life of Pope,* addressed to softies who might think the bad writers ridiculed in *The Dunciad* somehow unfairly maligned: "An author places himself uncalled before the tribunal of criticism," says Johnson, "and solicits fame at the hazard of disgrace." Or as E. M. Forster puts it:

Some reviews give pain. This is regrettable, but no author has the right to whine. He was not obliged to be an author. He invited publicity, and he must take the publicity that comes along.

Serious writers of all kinds—classic, romantic, ironic, even sentimental—understand the principle, and they understand it because you can't be a serious writer without deep moral awareness, even if you never let it show. Here's some perhaps unexpected wisdom from Edna St. Vincent Millay:

A person who publishes a book willfully appears before the populace with his pants down. . . . If it is a good book nothing can hurt him. If it is a bad book, nothing can help him.

John Keats is exemplary because he cared more for his work than for his publicity. When an acquaintance defended him from some bad reviews, he argued that defense was unnecessary and told him, "Praise or blame has but a momentary effect on the man whose love of beauty in the abstract makes him a severe critic of his own works." Note the distinctly premodern ring to that. Today it is the fantasy of celebrity, hardly the love of beauty, that seems to propel most aspirant writers—a term now all but equivalent to "novelists." Thus, unfavorable notices of their work offend deeply because they seem to proclaim their ineptitude to a wide paying audience, and it's a rare second- or third-rate writer who can resist immediately whipping off a letter to the review journal protesting the response his work has occasioned. Such a letter I have called an A.B.M., or Author's Big Mistake, since its effect is simply to reveal to an amused audience how deeply the author's feelings have been lacerated by the criticism he himself has so sedulously solicited. If the bad review has made him look like a ninny, his letter of outrage makes him look like an ass. What, then, is the author's appropriate recourse? Silence. His appropriate action? Getting busy on his next book immediately, and resolving this time to be as little elated by public praise as downcast by public blame.

In "Being Reviewed" I exhibited a handful of such letters and suggested that they constitute a new prose genre, new because so perfectly in tune with contemporary tendencies toward thin-skinned neurosis, egotism, and the consequent demand for favorable personal publicity. I naïvely supposed that my ridicule of these letters might reduce their number. But in the seven years since, authors' letters of grievance have, if anything, multiplied and grown more strident. Thus a further reprehension of this ethical indecency may be useful.

The dynamics of the author's angry letter are these. He or she reads the unfavorable review, which is of course a shock, since author, editor, family, and friends have been telling each other repeatedly how great this book is. Finding out there a stranger who doesn't think so, the author takes pen in hand and dashes off the letter of protest, quite forgetting Harry Truman's maxim "If you can't stand the heat, stay out of the kitchen." A whole taxonomy of literary vanity and its pathetic defense mechanisms is implicit in a sampling of these letters. (All the following, except the two indicated, come from that conspicuous enhancer of the middlebrow

Sunday-morning breakfast table, *The New York Times Book Review.*)

Sometimes you can stroke your vanity while pretending nobly to defend someone else's reputation. Reacting to a less-than-flattering review of his biography of an eminent scientist, one author performs an act of bogus generosity, declaring, "I am sad, not so much for myself, but for [the scientist]." He proceeds to gestures of stirring patriotism and disinterested public service: "The American people deserve to know about this man." How can they, he implies, when his book has been criticized? The reviewer, to be sure, is to blame, but even more culpable is the editor of the *Book Review,* who has "carelessly handed a scientific biography to a man ill equipped to review it." That is, unpersuaded to share the author's exalted view of it.

A standard maneuver of self-praise is to invoke the enthusiastic views of overwhelming thousands of honest readers, uncorrupted by the well-known cynicism and sadism of the book trade. Thus:

> To the Editor:
> I cannot shake my outrage at _____'s sneering review of _____. . . . Overwhelmingly readers have found it literate, absorbing, blazingly honest, sad, moving, humorous, full of *opera buffa* incidents and Runyonesque characters—and, above all, human. In short, a good read.

Every author his own reviewer, and every reviewer a blurb-writer.

Then there is the author's open embrace of the loser's precept, If others won't praise you, praise yourself:

To the Editor:

I am 55 years old. I have worked five days a week, 50 weeks a year, for over 30 years, as a novelist and poet. I set myself rather high standards: that unless the story is at once as unputdownable to a taxi driver as to a university professor, it is not good enough; that unless a novel is, at the end, quite clearly an epic poem, as well as a story, it is not good enough. My work has resulted in the publication of eight novels by 16 publishers. . . .

As an artist I thrive on criticism that emanates from knowledge of the work. . . . But Mr. _____'s criticisms come from without, not from knowing the book. . . .

Translation: to know me is to love me. (And one can note in passing the quality of that writer's perceptions: if he doesn't know that, in these days of Ph.D oversupply, a taxi-driver often *is* a university professor, his awareness of human nature and the social facts is probably not sufficient for a novelist.)

If someone doesn't think your book is as good as you do, there must be some hidden (and doubtless discreditable) motive. It is up to you to find it and disclose it to the public:

To the Editor:

_____ is, of course, perfectly entitled to say whatever he thinks about my book. . . . I find it strange, though, that among his generally withering comments he failed to mention that [my book] won the Thomas Cook Award for the best travel book of 1984, a competition in which the runners-up were those two considerable writers _____ and _____ and an understandably disappointed newcomer named _____[the reviewer].

It is also helpful to regard life, at least literary life, as a theater of melodrama in which, regardless of intellectual or aesthetic principles, revenges are taken and scores settled:

To the Editor:
_____'s unfavorable review of my novel . . . is curious in that it seems more an attack on me than on my book.
Readers perplexed by the strong ad hominem flavor of Mr. _____'s notice might be interested in knowing that in 1981 I wrote a highly unflattering critique of Mr. _____'s _____.
Could it be that Mr. _____ still rankles four years later?

And simple competitive and commercial jealousy can be made to account for many unfavorable views:

To the Editor:
I would like to comment on _____'s review of my book. . . . The reviewer's claim that there is little new

in it is not surprising, since Mr. _____ has, after all, a competing book of his own in the stores.

Another tack: if someone is not impressed by your book, you can always argue, or rather, assert, that he or she has not "understood" it. Upon consideration, however, this defense may seem hardly creditable, since, unlike a literary tyro, a publishing author has presumably learned to convey meaning and tone so precisely and with such control over the reader's responses that "misunderstandings" would appear to be his fault, not the reader's. Regardless, defense of the ground of *misunderstanding* is surely worth a try:

> To the Editor:
> It is clear, both from what _____ cites in his review of my novel . . . and from what he does not, that he did not get a handle on the virtuoso interplay of character, plot and theme that has struck other readers. Admittedly, _____ is a long, intricate novel. Reading it is a pleasure. Reviewing it, however, takes time and effort. . . . Mr. _____ wasn't up to it.

A nice line in self-praise there, too. As well as, we can be confident, in the lengthy document of rebuttal one aggrieved reviewee prepared to defend against the public's being misled by an unfavorable and in his view careless notice:

> To the Editors:
> . . . Mr. _____ does not like my book or me. . . .
> [He] writes that . . . "the first two pieces are chiefly im-

pressive in establishing that _____ is an unpleasant
man immensely alive.". . .

Anyone who wants to see the rather dreary account
of misquotations and foolish remarks in [the review] can
by writing to me at _____ and enclosing an addressed
and stamped envelope; and I will send them the long
answer . . . in the name of honesty.

(*The New York Review of Books*)

In my earlier bouquet of letters of this sort, I had thought
the all-time self-pity champion was the writer of the following:

Sir,—Your cruel review of my _____ reduced me to
tears, of course, as its author doubtless intended. . . .

(*Times Literary Supplement*)

Then, I despaired of coming upon a purer example. But it
seems true that literary genres are always moving toward
perfection—or exhaustion—by a heightening, even an exaggeration, of their most salient characteristics. Even in the
standard Author's Letter of Self-Pity a sort of generic progress occasioned by intensification can be discerned:

To the Editor:

I'm sure you receive many letters of dismay and
complaint over book reviews, and of course nothing is
perfect—still, how can I tell you how deeply you have

hurt me by publishing _____'s review of my new novel
. . . ? The degree of unfairness is what is so extreme, or,
believe me, I would not be sitting here feeling as if I have
witnessed the very authorities commit a terrible
crime. . . .

The book in question is one I worked on for more
than five years, and it came alive, and it does work—it
is relevant and it is compelling. . . . Yet you chose to give
it a short review, inconspicuously placed, and—and I
just cannot deal with this—your reviewer did not even
understand what he read. . . .

And you printed it. You break my heart. You owe
me much more than an apology.

The attentive reader will have noticed how many of these
pathetic egotists have been attracted to the business of writing *novels*. Is there something about the current state of that
literary form that allures especially the vainglorious, the neurotic, the self-important, the irrationally ambitious, the foolish? In that last letter, as so often, "unfairness" is charged,
which turns out to mean, as it does in the statement issued
by the Wharton School, that anyone who examines me and
my products dispassionately must arrive at the warmest admiration.

In my earlier encounter with this interesting subject, I
nominated the novelist and poet May Sarton as a prime
example of an author obsessed by her notices and their effect
upon her vanity. She was so cast down by abusive criticism
of her novels in *The New York Times Book Review* that she fell
into a deep funk lasting a whole year. "I felt like a deer shot

down by hunters," she declared, forgetting, while contriving that stagy metaphor, that the deer does not emerge from the privacy and silence of the woods, come to the edge, wag its antlers at the hunters, and invite them to take some shots. Ms. Sarton was so shaken by the experience of being shot down by literary opinion that she wrote a whole book about it, and anyone interested in the psychology of an author's vanity should read it: it is *Recovering: A Journal.*

But like the author of the former leading letter of self-pity, even May Sarton has now been overtaken. When he came to issue a new and augmented version of the *Dunciad,* Alexander Pope ordered Lewis Theobald, the mock-hero of the first version, "Utterly to vanish and evaporate out of this work," his place now to be occupied by Colley Cibber. In like manner, I now command May Sarton, the former Monarch of Auctorial Self-Pity, utterly to vanish from the precincts of this essay and to yield her place to a triumphant newcomer.

A perceptive Englishman once observed that there are some ideas so preposterous that only an educated person could believe them. Like, for example, Bertrand Russell, persuaded during the 1950s that the Americans were attempting to win the Korean War by dropping tainted bugs on the battlefield. No ordinary person, educated not at a high-class college but at a workman's bar, a sweatshop, an assembly line, or a secondary school of even minimal quality, could embrace for a moment the idea that sexual intercourse should be abjured entirely by women. So what if they like it? They shouldn't: it is an emblem of female subservience, and if women want babies, they can always have them without intercourse, by means of new biotechnologies. So what if sexual intercourse is one of the very few pleasures available to billions of women all over the world deprived by poverty and ignorance of most others? So what if intercourse is the way most women choose to express their love for their men? To hell with them all: they must give up intercourse because it is politically offensive.

Those are the suggestions of the self-styled radical feminist Andrea Dworkin (B.A., Bennington) in her book *Intercourse,* reviewed in *The New York Times Book Review* on May 3, 1987. The reviewer (naturally, some will say) thought Dworkin's idea absurd, the sort of vaporing that brings the feminist movement into severe discredit. She referred to Ms. Dworkin's argument as "this nonsense" and designated her book a "harangue" emanating from a flagrant "failure of imagination." The reviewer manages to avoid uttering a phrase like *ignorant puritanical zealot,* but she does suggest a telling analogy when she says of Ms. Dworkin's dream of an intercourseless world, "It's an appealing vision to fundamentalists of all persuasions, but it's wrong."

Encountering this reaction to her novel idea, Ms. Dworkin came alight and dashed off a letter of 450 words to the journal that had dared publish this critique. By this time, what with the precedents of the Dean of the Wharton School, Richard Nixon, and others, her starting by implicitly equating *fairly* with *favorably* will occasion little surprise:

To the Editor:
    I despair of being treated with respect, let alone fairly, in your pages. . . .

(An assumption worth noticing in passing is that editors determine the conclusions of reviewers. That assumption is one toward which the totalitarian personality naturally leans.)

> The review . . . is contemptuous beyond belief. . . . Your reviewer . . . seems to be functionally illiterate. . . . Your reviewer . . . did not condescend to mention any of the intellectual substance of the book. To do so would have interfered with the unbridled expression of contempt that seems to be the only acceptable attitude toward my work in New York literary circles. . . .

Aha, a conspiracy! and Ms. Dworkin closes with angry ethical instruction:

> I suggest you examine your ethics to see how you managed to avoid discussing anything real or even vaguely intelligent about my work and the political questions it raises.

(Notice the continued conflation of editor with reviewer in the last *you.*) There's a great deal that could be said about that letter, but one thing that's not at all clear is what reasons other than self-importance and power-hunger Ms. Dworkin has for expecting criticism to be more respectful toward her political ideas than to any other person's. Why does she demand that her ridiculous idea be treated with any less contempt than, say, Ronald Reagan's idea that there must be an end to the "exclusion of God" from the American classroom, or that Amtrak must be dissolved and passenger rail traffic returned to private hands, which means an utter end to it? Contempt for the contemptible, I say.

Although it might be going too far to assert that letting an unwelcome review pass without remonstrance is itself a sign of a serious writer as distinguished from a publicity hound or a neurotic show-off, it does appear that the authors who write in to object, argue, "clarify," "set the record straight," and correct misunderstandings of their works are rather consistently the hacks, amateurs, writers on the borders of vanity publishing, or those (like Andrea Dworkin) suffering under some personal defeat or sense of injured merit and anxious to bring a compensatory portentous message to erring humanity. They are very seldom writers whose concern is their craft, rather than their reputation or their impact on the universe.

We are left to contemplate the unpleasant facts good writers, like Orwell, recognize instinctively: that you aren't all that important; that no one cares terribly except yourself and your family whether your reputation is high or nonexistent; and that a book worth reading succeeds rather by word of mouth than by reviews, advertising, or dust-jacket blurbs. Good socialists, good university administrators, good presidents, and good writers are alike in this: they invite criticism, they don't fear it, and they certainly don't reject it, reserving the word *unfair* for bad calls at home plate.

KILLING,
IN
VERSE AND PROSE

A satire, says Samuel Johnson, is "a poem in which wickedness or folly is censured." This being so, Jon Stallworthy's *The Oxford Book of War Poetry* might just as well be titled *The Oxford Book of Satire*. In "No Man's Land," a poem by Eric Bogle, a skeptical young person sits by the grave of a nineteen-year-old killed in the First World War and addresses him thus:

Did you really believe that this war would end wars?
Well, the suffering, the sorrow, the glory, the shame,
The killing, the dying, it was all done in vain.
For, William McBride, it all happened again,
And again, and again, and again, and again.

That suggests the dynamics of Stallworthy's anthology. It
provides over and over, piling it very high and very deep,
material to gratify the harshest satirist of human nature and
of one mad institution people have devised to express themselves. Here a calumniator of humanity would find countless
sadistic mass murders and a sufficiency of needless agony and
bereavement, not to mention a plethora of stupid blunders,
failures of imagination, acts of ignorance, and egregious care-
lessness with the lives and bodies of others. There's also a lot
of fatuous complacency and optimism in the face of avoidable
catastrophe, as well as happiness in the misery of others, all
the way from the Hebrews' delight at the sufferings of Pha-
raoh's drowning cavalry and the bloody-mindedness of
Achilles to Seamus Heaney's notations of the murderous
absurdities in contemporary Ulster and Peter Porter's sardonic, scary take-off on a terminal nuclear civil-defense an-
nouncement. For the traducer of human nature, here is God's
plenty. Or rather, man's. As Byron puts it in *Don Juan,*

"Let there be light!" said God, and there was light!
"Let there be blood!" says man, and there's a sea.

Guiding the strong-stomached through this deplorable scene
is the British poet and translator who wrote the excellent

standard biography of the Great War poet Wilfred Owen
and went on to edit Owen's poems. He offers 259 poems,
and considering the difficulties of definition and classification
(not the least of which is that "war poetry" turns out to be
antiwar poetry, if not outright satire, in effect if not intention), he has done an OK job. He groups the poems chro-
nologically by war (surely a satiric nuance perceptible there?).
This has some disadvantages, like Thomas Hardy's appearing
in three different places: the Napoleonic Wars (a selection
from *The Dynasts),* the Boer War, and the Great War. For
this reason dates would be helpful, and there aren't half
enough of them, perhaps a reflection of the Oxford Book
tradition, going all the way back to Arthur Quiller-Couch's
original *Oxford Book of English Verse* (1900), that evidence of
precise scholarship is not the mark of a gentleman.

From Stallworthy's selections you can infer the outlines
of military as well as literary history. After the obligatory
Ancients, he provides a generous helping of the amazing Old
English war poems, like "The Battle of Maldon" and "The
Battle of Brunanburh," and a bit from Chaucer's "Knight's
Tale." He then displays examples of the chivalric swank with
which war is conventionally conceived in the Renaissance
among such as Spenser, Marvell, and Dryden. (Here some
might like a little Shakespeare as a counterweight to all this
grandiosity, something like Hotspur's speech from *Henry the
Fourth, Part I,* sneering at the staff-officer-like "administrator"
unacquainted with the unpleasant facts of the battlefield:

And as the soldiers bore dead bodies by,
He call'd them untaught knaves, unmannerly,

> To bring a slovenly unhandsome corse
> Betwixt the wind and his nobility.)

It's only with the onset of bourgeois understanding, in the eighteenth century, that poets begin reaching toward the modern theme that war is a total calamity rather than a welcome or not-too-bad occasion for displaying manliness. Only then does the idea begin to take form that victory is really defeat, as in Johnson's "The Vanity of Human Wishes" on the irony of Swedish Charles XII's "warrior's pride." His humiliation opens the door to an understanding of Napoleon's, Mussolini's, and Idi Amin's.

Coleridge, in "Fears in Solitude," is one of the first to reprehend military euphemisms ("all our dainty terms for fratricide"), which makes him an unexpected forerunner of Sassoon and e e cummings. And with Browning's "Incident of the French Camp" there enters another motif without which the antiwar poetry of the nineteenth and twentieth centuries would be sadly impoverished—tender, quasi-erotic fantasizing about the deaths of boy soldiers, as in Whitman's "Vigil Strange I Kept on the Field One Night," Rimbaud's "The Sleeper in the Valley," the works of Housman and Sir Henry Newbolt, and of course Wilfred Owen. Helping to flesh out Stallworthy's Civil War yield are four poems of Herman Melville's, which occasion the shock one always experiences upon seeing how badly a great writer can write:

> at my window, leaving bed,
> By night I mused, of easeful sleep bereft,
> On those brave boys (Ah War! thy theft) . . .

In this collection Kipling gets a fair shake. Stallworthy selects "Arithmetic on the Frontier," wonderfully "modern" in the irony with which it treats the expense of producing a young officer—all that training, all that costly equipment, all that practice ammunition, all those uniforms and quarters and officers-club amenities—and the inexpensive ease with which he is destroyed:

The Crammer's boast, the Squadron's pride,
Shot like a rabbit in a ride!

There's plenty of irony too in Stallworthy's selections from Hardy and Housman on the Boer War, as well, of course, as in the well-known poems of the Great War.

On the other hand, the poems from the Spanish Civil War seem uniformly unsatisfactory. What's the reason? Was their audience too narrow politically, too much a faction? Was it too philistine? Were the poets too self-righteous for irony? Was sophisticated technique conceived to be inappropriate in a "people's war"? That is, was good writing itself thought offensively privileged and suspect, even "Fascist"? Whatever the reason, the Spanish War poems, by John Cornford, Laurie Lee, Auden and Spender and Bernard Spencer, seem to take their places in this collection less because they're good than because the book requires the display of work from each major "conflict" (Stallworthy's euphemism).

In representing poems from the Second World War, Stallworthy has been fair, offering both highminded performances in which remnants òf a chivalric understanding may be detected (like some poems by Keith Douglas) and examples of the pissed-off, the demotic, snotty, and nay-saying. Henry Reeds's classic "Lessons of the War" is included, of course, and so is Gavin Ewart's wonderful "When a Beau Goes In" and John Pudney's "To Johnny." I wish Pudney's "Missing" were here too, for in its minimalism, its resolute disinclination to go on and on or to try to interpret the uninterpretable, it is so memorable a registration of the quintessential style of the Second World War. Of the events of that calamity, less said the better:

      MISSING
Less said the better.
The bill unpaid, the dead letter,
No roses at the end
Of Smith, my friend.

Last words don't matter,
And there are none to flatter.
Words will not fill the post
Of Smith, the ghost.

For Smith, our brother,
Only son of loving mother,
The ocean lifted, stirred,
Leaving no word.

That little twelve-line notation is worth attending to because it is so efficiently emblematic of the verbal culture of the Second World War as contrasted with that of the First.

For participants, the Second War was silent. Not that the explosions made less noise. Rather, no one felt it appropriate to say much, either to try to interpret the war, or to understand it, or even to execrate it. It was simply there, taking place, and there seemed nothing to say. Contrast the troops' flux of talk in the First World War, their constant bringing of language to bear on the war, their unremitting verbalizing, caught nicely in David Jones's long poem *In Parenthesis*. The high-minded loquacity of all those poets of the Great War! Entirely a different scene from the style of the Second War, which is silence—silence ranging from the embarrassed to the sullen. It's as if both the ironic and the elegiac conventions for making some literary sense of modern war had been exhausted earlier. Result: a new laconic style.

In the Civil War, by contrast again, it was appropriate for soldiers on both sides to be noisily enthusiastic. As the officer of an Illinois unit reported of his men, "On the march they make it a point to abuse every man or thing they see." And of an Indiana regiment a survivor remembers:

Our regiment yelled at everything they saw and heard. When another regiment passed, they yelled at them. . . . As they tumbled out to roll-call in the morning, they yelled. . . . After a hard day's scouting they were never too tired to hail the end of their tasks with a joyous yell. . . . A yell would start at one end of the division, and regiment after regiment and brigade after brigade would take it up and carry it along, and then send it back to the other end; few knowing what it was about, and caring less.

But as the military commentator S. L. A. Marshall has perceived, the Second World War produced "about the mutest army we ever sent to war," an army unwilling to waste its breath on exhortations, noisy encouragements, yelling for the fun of it, or even much conversation. Thus in the Second War a bomber navigator hearkens to the silence that overcomes his aircrew waiting for the start of a mission: "Remember that bit in *Journey's End*," he says, "where the older man engages the younger in a discussion about tea and cocoa as beverages while they talk away the last moments of their lives?" In contrast, he observes, "We usually wait in silence." And virtually in silence too the airmen returned from their missions, most notably when their friends' planes did not. Then, after their interrogation, some of the survivors were likely to assemble in someone's barracks room, open a bottle of whiskey, and sit around wordlessly until one might offer a quiet minimalist toast to the code designation of the missing plane but without specifying anyone's name. He would raise his glass and say very softly, "God bless 'M for Momsie.' " And they would drink and then go about their business. As one airman remembers, "You learned to keep emotion at a very low level."

Pudney's laconic enactment of the bankruptcy of elegy takes place in 55 words only. Compare the 312 words Julian Grenfell needs—or rather uses—to deliver the cheering news of his Great War poem "Into Battle." This assures the reader that, unlike the wordlessness of Pudney's ocean, the elements of nature conspire to say a great deal, speaking to the soldier constant encouraging words:

The woodland trees that stand together,
   They stand to him each one a friend;
They gently speak in the windy weather;
   They guide to valley and ridge's end.

The kestrel hovering by day,
   And the little owls that call by night,
Bid him be swift and keen as they,
   As keen of ear, as swift of sight.

The blackbird sings to him, etc., etc.

No one and no thing verbalizes so lavishly in the memorable poems of the Second World War. An American counterpart of Pudney's "Missing" is Randall Jarrell's "The Death of the Ball Turret Gunner," which needs only five lines for its understated work. Second World War poetry is so notably an art of litotes that one can almost gauge the merit and staying power of a poem by its brevity. If it's short and small, like Pudney's and Jarrell's, it may be good. If long and large, like, say, Karl Shapiro's "Elegy for a Dead Soldier," probably not. In that war even the voluble, indeed musical, Dylan Thomas feels a certain tug in the direction of silence, registering in one title "A Refusal to Mourn . . ." and declining to expend a load of words memorializing "the Death, by Fire, of a Child in London."

But it is in Jarrell's poem that one sees the Second War

poetic action in its essence. The speaker in the poem, the
dead gunner, abjures syntax betokening cause and coherence.
He is either disinclined or simply unable to do more than
specify serially the crazy things that have happened to him.
Understanding his experience is as far from his capacity as
interpreting it. And he certainly does not object to it. ("I
made no comment. / What should I resent?"):

From my mother's sleep I fell into the State,
And I hunched in its belly till my wet fur froze.
Six miles from earth, loosed from its dream of life,
I woke to black flak and the nightmare fighters.
When I died they washed me out of the turret with a
    hose.

If it might be possible to assign a cause to the Second World
War, it would not be easy to infer a meaning. When we hear
the phrase *war poetry,* we probably think of the poetry of the
First, not the Second War. Indeed, at this distance it's not
hard to sense behind most of the Allied writing of the Second
War the shade of what Susan Sontag will later designate,
speaking of Pinter's plays, "The Aesthetics of Silence." The
banality I've noted in the writings of the O.W.I. generation
is designed to fill a vacuum, the empty space left because
there is nothing to say. V. S. Pritchett recalls one of Elizabeth
Bowen's characters observing of the London blitz, "It will
have no literature." "In that sense," says Pritchett, "it was
like a car smash or pile-up."

After silence and failure of understanding, anxiety and shame, as in Howard Nemerov's "Redeployment":

They say the war is over. But water still
Comes bloody from the taps, and my pet cat
In his disorder vomits worms which crawl
Swiftly away. . . .

That seems to prepare for the next acts: Korea, Vietnam, Lebanon, Northern Ireland, the Falklands, Grenada, and Nicaragua, the last three too recent to have produced their appropriate satirists.

And speaking of Vietnam, how is it that we know ("for certain," it's tempting to add) that no weighty, sustained poems, or even short poems of distinction, are going to come out of it? Why do we expect from it nothing like, say, Herbert Read's "The End of a War," from the Great War, or Louis Simpson's "The Runner," from the Second? Why are we sure that in a back room somewhere no one is writing the equivalent of Isaac Rosenberg's "Break of Day in the Trenches" or Jarrell's "Eighth Air Force"? Is it perhaps that we secretly recognize that real poetry is, as Hazlitt called it, "right royal," aristocratic in essence, and thus unlikely to arise from the untutored or the merely street-smart? (Here, I'm noting how few literary or highly educated people were in that war, how few who had any chance in their high schools to experience real poetry or to gain any sense of how one might write it.) Or is the reason for the paucity of Vietnam war poetry a fact even more unpleasant, namely, that we are now inescapably mired in a postverbal age, where neither writer nor reader possesses the layers of allusion arising from wide literary experience that make significant writing and reading possible? Or is the reason our despair of urging public events toward any "meaning," arising from the suspicions of traditional value that have encouraged "deconstruction" in criticism and "Marxism" in the daydreams of those at once intelligent and powerless? Whatever the reasons, it seems undeniable that no one expects interesting poetry to emerge from that sad war. All we can expect is more of what we have, a few structureless free-verse dribbles of easy irony or easy sentiment or easy political anger. Some samples are in Stallworthy's book, and they are not good, even though written by Denise Levertov and Galway Kinnell.

Indeed, there are many bad poems in his book, perhaps an indication that if you accumulate poems by their themes or subjects, very soon (unless the theme is mortality or evanescence) you're going to be in artistic trouble. It's a sad comment that most of the mediocre poems in Stallworthy's collection come from the twentieth century. I don't mean the readily patronized patriotic Great War pieces by adolescents like Rupert Brooke and Herbert Asquith. Such naïve documents are landmarks in the history of sensibility and one expects to find them in a collection like this. Rather, I mean items like Allen Tate's once-fashionable Eliotic "Ode to the Confederate Dead," which now seems embarrassingly bogus, inert, and unnecessary, as well as poems like Paul Dehn's heartwarming but shallow "St. Aubin d'Aubigné" and Auden's would-be resolute but flaccid "Spain, 1937." The sad fact is that there aren't really enough good "war poems" that

succeed as poems to make a book of more than 350 pages.
Stallworthy has thus had to pad out with things like Edith
Sitwell's preposterous, theologically pretentious "Still Falls
the Rain," that implausible theatrical farrago which seems
now the very *locus classicus* of 1940s empty portentousness.

That Sitwellian disaster prompts this question: why
haven't more women written good "war poems"? From Homer's Andromache to Vera Brittain (and the "Mrs. Smith"
of Pudney's "Missing") bereaved women, next to the per-
manently disabled, are the main victims in war, their dead
having been removed beyond suffering and memory to the
place where, as Gavin Ewart puts it,

     there falls no rain nor hail nor driven snow—
Here, there, or anywhere,

and thus

Do you suppose *they* care?

Yet the elegies are written by men, many of them as "noncombatant" as the women, and poems registering a love of
soldiers are written by men, and it's not women who seem
the custodians of the subtlest sorts of antiwar irony. This
seems odd, and it awaits interpretation.

Any student of antiwar irony must wonder how much and
what sort attaches to the quotation marks around Studs

Terkel's title *"The Good War."* Even skeptics who think "oral history" better designated "oral fiction" or "oral self-justification" are likely to be impressed by Terkel's book, which exhibits again his talent for eliciting significant emotion from the people he talks to. In essence he is asking his interviewees who were "in" the Second World War in various ways, whether the ironic quotes belong around the title. With rare patience and sympathy he has conversed with more than a hundred "ordinary" people: former servicemen, housewives, businessmen, and girlfriends, and not just those on our side but Germans and Japanese, and such curious Allies as Russians as well. And some of his testifiers are a cut above the ordinary: Mayor Tom Bradley of Los Angeles, Pauline Kael, John Ciardi, John Kenneth Galbraith, Marcel Ophuls, Maxine Andrews (of the harmonic Sisters), Roosevelt's assistant Tommy "The Cork" Corcoran, Averell Harriman, John Houseman, the cartoonist Milton Caniff (*Terry and the Pirates*), Telford Taylor, and Bill Mauldin (can that impudent little GI really now be a bearded sixty-five-year-old?).

"The past is never dead," Faulkner once said. "It's not even past." Many of Terkel's informants broke down in sobs while recalling their war experience forty years back. Of course, war trauma being one of our dirty little secrets, always there beneath the surface, seldom showing except on occasions like this. Terkel has not merely got his people to talk frankly and poignantly. He has edited the results with laudable sense and humanity to produce a striking indictment of American policy in the postwar world, and the popularity of his book suggests widespread approval of an attitude about that war and its aftermath which is powerfully opposed to the official one.

While there are still some who will go to their graves hating the enemy and resolutely not buying Sonys and Volkswagens, a lot of pity for the other side has surfaced after all these years. One former soldier who fought in Europe remembers his shock at discovering that the dead German infantry "were exactly our age. . . . Once the helmet is off, you're looking at a teenager, another kid." A soldier who found himself in Japan just after the surrender recalls a sudden perception after a Japanese father-in-law showed him a picture of a "missing" Japanese soldier: "It dawned on me that they suffered the same as we did. They lost sons and daughters and relatives, and they hurt too."

Others, like the sensitive and honest ex-Marine E. B. Sledge, find the horror unforgettable. He recalls vividly what he wishes more people knew about, the savagery of island fighting in the Pacific, with American lads turning into virtual animals, routinely murdering the Japanese wounded, smashing the faces of corpses to get at the gold teeth. "How could American boys do this?" he asks, and answers, "We *were* savages." Those attentive at once to Golding's *Lord of the Flies* and the data of the Holocaust (as well as the behavior of our troops in Vietnam) will readily understand. In order to "make any sense" at all of the Holocaust, says Marguerite Duras, we must recognize that we could have done all those terrible things ourselves. "We must share the crime." It must be conceived not in German or Nazi but "in world terms" and "understood collectively." *We* did it. "If you give a German and not a collective interpretation to the Nazi horror, you reduce the man in Belsen to regional dimensions. The only possible answer to this crime is to turn it into a crime committed by everyone. To share it." Which means that if you can't imagine yourself an SS officer hustling the Jewish women and children to the gas chamber, you need to be more closely in touch with your buried self.

But if there's guilt here, there's pathos too. Some of Terkel's speakers indicate the war's cost to the unfortunates whose destiny it was to constitute the cutting edge in the now-forgotten ominous places. A former airman in the South Pacific shows Terkel a photograph of a squadron baseball team:

At first base we had Max and O'Connell; they used to alternate. Both those men died at Cananatuan. . . . At shortstop we had Armando Viselli. . . . Armando died in a reconnaissance flight over Lamon Bay. . . . At third base was Cabbage Clan. . . . He died when his ship was torpedoed off Mindinao . . . by a U.S. Navy submarine. We had two Catchers. We had Beck. He was hit on the first day the Japanese bombed at Clark Field and his leg was badly mangled. . . . The other catcher was Dumas. He was from Massachusetts. Dumas was killed on the first day at Iba. I'm the only one left out of the whole infield, the only one that came back. That's why I treasure that picture.

There is much in Terkel's book about injustice, and not just the inevitable injustice of the unlucky few bearing the awful burden for the many. The notion that the war was a notable moral crusade will hardly survive the testimony about home-front anti-Semitism, much of it found in the Junior-Leaguish Red Cross. "We're supposed to be against Hitler," one woman recalls, "yet we were talking anti-Jew all the time. " And the idea that the war was "against Fascism" is embarrassed by the unpleasant facts of rampant racism at home, where it was assumed that blacks were cowards by birth and incompetents by instinct, incapable of flying a plane without an accident or manning a front line without running away. Segregation was rigid, and as one Red Cross worker remembers, "Until we were well into the war, they segregated the blood plasma of the blacks from the whites."

Other memories convey the sense of a period so far back as to be, now, virtually not understandable without great effort. It's not easy to call back a living sense of that pre-pill, pre-porno, pre-abortion world of puritanism and inhibition, when *Esquire* was thought racy, in trouble constantly with the Postmaster General for its sexy drawings, and when a girl could imperil her future by establishing a reputation for being "fast." "There was very little sleeping around," says a girl who was living on the West Coast. "We were still at the tail-end of a moral generation. Openly living together was not condoned."

That girl's name was Dellie Hahne, and she is now only one of many here who register the utmost life-distorting disillusion with the way the postwar world has turned out. The rearming of the Germans and the rapid reversal of the wartime party line toward the Soviet Union were shocks from which many will never recover. The United States government has forfeited the credibility and respect of more people than it knows, and the vein of distrust and cynicism about national purposes runs very deep. Vietnam and Watergate and the Iran-contra perversion are only the latest in a series of debilitating events that date from 1945, when the OSS was transformed into the CIA and the basis established for a secret government on a military model. "When we started to arm Germany," says Dellie Hahne, "I was so shocked. I'd been sold a bill of goods. . . . That was the beginning of distrusting my own government."

Pervasive also is the anti-militarism of these reminiscences. An atomic physicist says, "We can't afford to be weak. That's what the Germans said. And did. . . . Look what happened to them. The same thing will happen to us if we don't cool it." Retired Admiral Gene LaRoque spills beans formerly out of sight but now abundantly visible since the Iran-contra business: "Our military runs our foreign policy. The State Department simply goes around and tidies up the messes the military makes." The United States still tends to see things in terms of the war, LaRoque points out, and the memory of the "Victory"—and subsequent papering over of the agony and the cost—"encourages the men of my generation to be willing, almost eager, to use military force anywhere in the world." An Englishwoman who survived the Blitz says of Americans, "I do wish they wouldn't be so keen to get into wars, because one day it will come back on your territory and God help you."

A former artillery officer, a forward observer at the battle of the Huertgen Forest near the German border, remembers: "I knew another forward observer. He went out with his crew. White phosphorus was thrown at him. Two of the men burned before his eyes. He came running to where I was. . . . I went down the road to meet him. He was sobbing and falling into my arms. He kept saying, 'No more killing, no more killing, no more killing.' " A rational humanity, which is what we have not got, would have no trouble ratifying that resolution.

James Jones and his son, together with Willie Morris and his son (both boys fifteen years old), once visited the battlefield at Antietam. The four of them walked down the Sunken Road, which just after the battle was known as Bloody Lane. Morris recalls the history of the place:

Here, along a line of a thousand yards, the Confederate center took its stand, thousands of them firing at close quarters against the Federal troops charging across the crest of a ridge. It lasted three hours. And the dead Confederate soldiers lay so thick here that as far as the eye could see a man could walk upon them without once touching ground.

At the end of the Sunken Road is an observation tower. From its top the two men and the two boys surveyed the silent landscape.

"The way men go to die," Jim said, looking down at the ridge before us. "It's incredibly sad. It breaks my heart.

You wonder why it was necessary, why human beings
have to do that to each other. . . ."

Why do men do it, one of the boys wondered.
Why did they do it here?

After thinking a while how to answer that question of questions, Jones gave the simple, empirical, irrational answer any
ex-soldier would authenticate. They did it, said Jones, "because they didn't want to appear unmanly in front of their
friends." Considering the constant fresh supply of young men
and the universal young man's need for assurance of his
manhood, Jones's answer suggests why reason, decency, and
common sense are as unlikely to stop the killing in the future
as in the past. Animals and trees and stones cannot be sati-
rized, only human beings, and that's the reason it's all going
to happen again, and again, and again, and again.

A WELL-REGULATED
MILITIA

In the spring Washington swarms with high school graduating classes. They come to the great pulsating heart of the Republic—which no one has yet told them is Wall Street —to be impressed by the White House and the Capitol and the monuments and the Smithsonian and the space capsules. Given the state of public secondary education, I doubt if many of these young people are at all interested in language and rhetoric, and I imagine few are fascinated by such attendants of power and pressure as verbal misrepresentation and disingenuous quotation. But any who are can profit from a stroll past the headquarters of the National Rifle Association of America, its slick marble façade conspicuous at 1600 Rhode Island Avenue, NW.

There they would see an entrance flanked by two marble panels offering language, and language more dignified and traditional than that customarily associated with the Association's gun-freak constituency, with its T-shirts reading GUNS, GUTS, AND GLORY ARE WHAT MADE AMERICA GREAT and its belt buckles proclaiming I'LL GIVE UP MY GUN WHEN THEY PRY MY COLD DEAD FINGERS FROM AROUND IT. The marble panel on the right reads, "The right of the people to keep and bear arms shall not be infringed," which sounds familiar. So familiar that the student naturally expects the left-hand panel to honor the principle of symmetry by presenting the first half of the quotation, namely: "A well-regulated Militia, being necessary to the security of a free state, . . ." But looking to the left, the inquirer discovers not that clause at all but rather this lame list of NRA functions and specializations: "Firearms Safety Education. Marksmanship Training. Shooting for Recreation." It's as if in presenting its well-washed, shiny public face the NRA doesn't want to remind anyone of the crucial dependent clause of the Second Amendment, whose latter half alone it is so fond of invoking to urge its prerogatives. (Some legible belt buckles of members retreat further into a seductive vagueness, reading only, "Our American Heritage: the Second Amendment.") We infer that for the Association, the less emphasis on the clause about the militia, the better. Hence its pretense on the front of its premises that the quoted main clause is not crucially dependent on the now unadvertised subordinate clause—indeed, it's meaningless without it.

Because flying .38- and .45-caliber bullets rank close to cancer, heart disease, and AIDS as menaces to public health in this country, the firearm lobby, led by the NRA, comes under liberal attack regularly, and with special vigor immediately after an assault on some conspicuous person like Ronald Reagan or John Lennon. Thus *The New Republic,* in April 1981, deplored the state of things but offered as a solution only the suggestion that the whole Second Amendment be perceived as obsolete and amended out of the Constitution. This would leave the NRA with not a leg to stand on.

But here as elsewhere a better solution would be not to fiddle with the Constitution but to take it seriously, the way we've done with the First Amendment, say, or with the Thirteenth, the one forbidding open and avowed slavery. And by taking the Second Amendment seriously I mean taking it literally. We should "close read" it and thus focus lots of attention on the grammatical reasoning of its two clauses. This might shame the NRA into pulling the dependent clause out of the closet, displaying it on its façade, and accepting its not entirely pleasant implications. These could be particularized in an Act of Congress providing:

(1) that the Militia shall now, after these many years, be "well regulated," as the Constitution requires.

(2) that any person who has chosen to possess at home a gun of any kind, and who is not a member of the police or the military or an appropriate government agency, shall be deemed to have enrolled automatically in the Militia of the United States. Members of the Militia, who will be issued

identifying badges, will be organized in units of battalion, company, or platoon size representing counties, towns, or boroughs. If they bear arms while not proceeding to or from scheduled exercises of the Militia, they will be punished "as a court martial may direct."

(3) that any gun owner who declines to join the regulated Militia may opt out by selling his firearms to the federal government for $1,000 each. He will sign an undertaking that if he ever again owns firearms he will be considered to have enlisted in the Militia.

(4) that because the Constitution specifically requires that the Militia shall be "well regulated," a regular training program, of the sort familiar to all who have belonged to military units charged with the orderly management of small arms, shall be instituted. This will require at least eight hours of drill each Saturday at some convenient field or park, rain or shine or snow or ice. There will be weekly supervised target practice (separation from the service, publicly announced, for those who can't hit a barn door). And there will be ample practice in digging simple defense works, like foxholes and trenches, as well as necessary sanitary installations like field latrines and straddle trenches. Each summer there will be a six-week bivouac (without spouses), and this, like all the other exercises, will be under the close supervision of long-service noncommissioned officers of the United States Army and the Marine Corps. On bivouac, liquor will be forbidden under extreme penalty, but there will be an issue every Friday night of two cans of 3.2 beer, and feeding will follow traditional military lines, the cuisine consisting largely of shit-on-a-shingle, sandwiches made of bull dick (baloney) and choke-ass (cheese), beans, and fatty pork. On

Sundays and holidays, powdered eggs for breakfast. Chlorinated water will often be available, in Lister Bags. Further obligatory exercises designed to toughen up the Militia will include twenty-five-mile hikes and the negotiation of obstacle courses. In addition, there will be instruction of the sort appropriate to other lightly armed, well-regulated military units: in map-reading, the erection of double-apron barbed-wire fences, and the rudiments of military courtesy and the traditions of the Militia, beginning with the Minute Men. Per diem payments will be made to those participating in these exercises.

(5) that since the purpose of the Militia is, as the Constitution says, to safeguard "the security of a free state," at times when invasion threatens (perhaps now the threat will come from Nicaragua, national security no longer being menaced by North Vietnam) all units of the Militia will be trucked to the borders for the duration of the emergency, there to remain in field conditions (here's where the practice in latrine-digging pays off) until Congress declares that the emergency has passed. Congress may also order the Militia to perform other duties consistent with its constitutional identity as a regulated volunteer force: for example, flood and emergency and disaster service (digging, sandbag filling, rescuing old people); patrolling angry or incinerated cities; or controlling crowds at large public events like patriotic parades, motor races, and professional football games.

(6) that failure to appear for these scheduled drills, practices, bivouacs, and mobilizations shall result in the Militiaperson's dismissal from the service and forfeiture of badge, pay, and firearm.

.   .   .   .

Why did the Framers of the Constitution add the word *bear* to the phrase "keep and bear arms"? Because they conceived that keeping arms at home implied the public obligation to bear them in a regulated way for "the security of" not a private household but "a free state." If interstate bus fares can be regulated, it is hard to see why the Militia can't be, especially since the Constitution says it must be. *The New Republic* has recognized that "the Second Amendment to the Constitution clearly connects the right to bear arms to the 18th-century national need to raise a militia." But it goes on: "That need is now obsolete, and so is the amendment." And it concludes: "If the only way this country can get control of firearms is to amend the Constitution, then it's time for Congress to get the process under way."

I think not. Rather, it's time not to amend Article II of the Bill of Rights (and Obligations) but to read it, publicize it, embrace it, and enforce it. That the Second Amendment stems from concerns that can be stigmatized as "18th-century" cuts little ice. The First Amendment stems precisely from such concerns, and no one but Yahoos wants to amend it. Also "18th-century" is that lovely bit in Section 9 of Article I forbidding any "Title of Nobility" to be granted by the United States. That's why we've been spared Lord Annenberg and Sir Leonard Bernstein, Knight. Thank God for the eighteenth century, I say. It understood not just what a firearm is and what a Militia is. It also understood what "well regulated" means. It knew how to compose a constitutional article and it knew how to read it. And it assumed that everyone, gun lobbyists and touring students alike, would understand and correctly quote it. Both halves of it.

TRAVEL, TOURISM, AND "INTERNATIONAL UNDERSTANDING"

Question: I am planning a trip to Hong Kong but do not like Chinese food. Are there any restaurants that serve American-type meals?

—S.K., Brooklyn

S.K. is clearly not a traveler but a tourist, and a tourist of the grossest kind, and yet it was in the "Travel" section of a large, not unintelligent metropolitan newspaper that S.K.'s letter recently appeared. If S.K.'s problem comes under the head of "Travel," clearly some interesting things involving language and behavior are going on.

Those whose goal it is to insulate people from the foreign and to move them around profitably in large groups hope to persuade them that the terms *tourism* and *travel* are synonymous. Similarly, those whose goal it is to sell domestic dwellings hope to persuade their patsies that a *house* and a *home* are identical, and thus advertise "a lovely quarter-of-a-million-dollar home." But since a *housewrecker* differs significantly from a *homewrecker,* the inference is clear that *house* and *home* mean different things, although the new gentility and sentimentality, issuing in the new euphemism, labor constantly to efface the difference. The *Philadelphia Inquirer* has spoken recently of boarding homes, and it will probably not be long before we hear of whorehomes, homes of prostitution, and bawdy homes. Will publishing houses finally be known as publishing homes, whose authors will be urged to follow, in their writing mechanics, home style?

Despite cunning attempts to insinuate the identity of travel and tourism, the fact that S.K.'s question, when it appears in a Travel context, is perceived to verge on the comic suggests that there is a difference, and it's a difference some still think important. It may be worth noting that the publishers of the French Michelin Green Guides label them Tourist Guides, while over here the publishers of the Fodor Guides call them, shrewdly, Travel Guides. I don't want to suggest that Europeans have a special lien on honest dealing, only that they are sometimes better at facing than euphemizing embarrassing realities, if not unpleasant facts. The *bidet* is a case in point.

Of course tourism and travel do have a lot in common, which is why it's not hard for the industry to confound them. Both are mechanisms of escape—from the daily, the job, the boss, even the parents, as Freud observes: "A great part of the pleasure of travel," he says, "lies in the fulfillment of early wishes to escape the family and especially the father." Both also permit a form of escape from one's customary identity, for among total strangers it is tempting and not too difficult to try on a new selfhood or new disguises. Lévi-Strauss observes that because most travel or tourism takes you to places more ancient than home, you move not just in space but in time as well. And you move socially too: Lévi-Strauss has noticed repeatedly that arriving in some new place he has suddenly, like a character in a fairy tale, become rich. (Visitors to Mexico, India, or China will know the feeling.)

Travelers and tourists are also alike to the degree that they are achieving relief from the same thing—the ugliness and racket of Western cities, from factories, parking lots, boring turnpikes, and roadside squalor. Indeed, every tourist-advertising come-on constitutes an implicit satire on the terrible modern scene, testifying to the universal longing to flee into some version of pastoral. And naturally the most "advanced" environments prove in experience the most loathsome, providing maximum impulses to flight. As Nancy Mitford has observed, "North Americans very naturally want to get away from North America."

Travel and tourism have another thing in common. They both convey the pleasure of learning new things, and it's in the joy of learning that even explorers resemble in small part tourists and travelers. Explorers are pleased to learn the contours of unknown shorelines and the existence of novel flora and fauna. Tourists delight in mastering exchange rates and learning where to go in Paris for a really good burger with fries—or in Hong Kong for good old American cooking. Travelers find equal happiness in mastering foreign customs and manners and encountering curious cuisines and experiencing "odd" beliefs and unfamiliar forms of government.

And there's one further place tourism and travel converge. Both, as Jonathan Culler points out, involve quests for authenticity, and it's this that distinguishes both from exploration. Because authenticity is measured by a thing's being identified as a pure example of the known, or even the cliché, the traveler is not so easily distinguished from the tourist as most who conceive themselves travelers like to think. Both journey in search of something considered more authentic than what the home scene can offer. A "pure" or "real" traveler would probably go in search of nothing nameable: he would simply wander, approximating an absolute *flâneur*. And Culler goes on to observe that "one of the characteristics of modernity is the belief [as registered, for example, in *The Waste Land* and similar artifacts] that authenticity has somehow been lost, that it exists only in the past . . . or else in other regions or countries." Thus, says Dean MacCannell, a notable theorist of tourism, for the American tourist or traveler "The United States makes the rest of the world seem authentic. California makes the rest of the United States ['New England' is an example] seem authentic." And quoting this, Culler adds, perhaps too cruelly, "Los Angeles makes the rest of California seem authentic."

But there, in their common quest for "authenticity," resemblances between tourism and real travel virtually run out, and we are reduced to facing their glaring differences. For one thing, tourism is unlikely to offer an equivalent to the psychological and emotional intensity of travel. To travel is to sharpen remarkably the experience of the senses: you feel, hear, and see things with abnormal clarity and force. Like the quintessential traveler D. H. Lawrence one cold morning in Sardinia, finding "wonderful" the simple feeling of standing alone on a strange road:

> Wonderful to go out on a frozen road. . . . Wonderful the bluish, cold air, and things standing up in cold distance. . . . I am so glad, on this lonely naked road, I don't know what to do with myself.

Lord Byron knew the travel feeling, for he held that "the great object of life is . . . to feel that we exist," and he found that sensation in three things especially: gambling, battle, and travel, all, he says, "intemperate but keenly felt pursuits . . . whose principal attraction is the agitation inseparable from their accomplishment." (Odd that he omits *love* from this triad, but perhaps it's implied under *gambling* and *battle*.) And the deeply romantic emotion attending real travel has been felt memorably by Paul Bowles, always searching for a "magic place" which will yield its secrets and grant the seeker, finally, "wisdom and ecstasy."

As a form of intensified, heightened experience, travel differs from tourism in being not relaxing and comfortable and consoling. The word of course derives from *travail,* and travel is less like the vacationing which tourism resembles than like a quest for a new kind of strenuousness. It is a laborious adventure amidst strange evil as well as strange good. One of the traveler's ailments is homesickness, and another is loneliness. And a customary, if not always admitted, companion is fear—of strangers, of embarrassment, of violence or madness appearing in unaccustomed forms. Albert Camus properly distinguishes travel from tourism when he perceives that

> what gives value to travel is fear. It breaks down a kind of inner structure we have. One can no longer cheat— hide behind the hours spent at the office or at the plant. . . . Travel robs us of such refuge. Far from our own people, our own language, stripped of all our props, deprived of our masks (one doesn't know the fare of the streetcars, or anything else), we are completely on the surface of ourselves.

"But also," he adds, "we restore to every being and every object its miraculous value." There's undeniably something of the miraculous and mysterious about travel, and miracles are not mass-produced.

"The age of independent travel is drawing to an end," said E. M. Forster back in 1920, when it had been increasingly clear for decades that the mass production inevitable in the late-industrial age had generated its own travel-spawn, tourism, which is to travel as plastic is to wood. If travel is mysterious, even miraculous, and often lonely and frightening, tourism is commonsensical, utilitarian, safe, and social, "that gregarious passion," the traveler Patrick Leigh Fermor calls it, "which destroys the object of its love." Not self-directed but externally enticed, as a tourist you go not where your own curiosity beckons but where the industry has decreed you shall go. Tourism soothes, shielding you from the shocks of novelty and menace, confirming your prior view of the world rather than shaking it up. It obliges you not just to behold conventional things but to behold them in the approved conventional way. The objects most often miniaturized and vended as souvenirs indicate the indispensable Holy Grails of tourism: the Eiffel Tower, Mount Fuji, the Statue of Liberty, all desirable not because of their beauty, magic, or eccentricity but because of their familiarity. "Sight sacralization" is the term MacCannell applies to this touristic process of simplifying some presumed national identity and reducing it to a handy bit of portable, salable shorthand. And such tourist clichés don't even have to remain *in situ*. Busch Gardens, an entertainment park near Williamsburg, Virginia, simulates not just the architecture of well-known places in France, Italy, and Germany, but the street scenes, the music, the crowds, and the folk events. "Why go to Europe," it advertises, "when you can get it all at Busch Gardens?"

The great principle of industrial mediocrity and uniformity is, "Unless everybody wants it, nobody gets it." That is the inviolable rule of mass tourism, the same rule governing such other group experiences as mass feeding and mass education. Anathema to all these is the conviction of the sacredness of individuals (like such travelers as Robert Byron or Eric Newby or Rebecca West). Impatient of their kind of fructive oddity and their rampant wills, tourism assumes total docility in its clients. It knows that actuality will disappoint them unless interpreted on the spot by some authority. Thus the tourist is at all times attended by his guides, couriers, and tour directors, lecturing at him, telling him things, and assiduously insulating him from abroad, its surprises, mysteries, and threats. The "personalities" of these attendants, furthermore, are presumed to be a significant part of the appeal of group touring. As one tour company advertised recently, its guides "have bright, witty personalities, and love to share anecdotes and chit-chat with the family." Another company makes the point that its guides are more than guides: they are "entertainers." (A long distance, this, from the ideal of Baedeker, whose devotees used to travel largely to escape from things like that and who relied on the Baedeker guidebooks precisely to liberate them from such intrusions.) In addition, the tourist is wholly protected from contingency, which might be taken to mean protected from life. By contrast, the traveler, as Patrick White has noticed, often arrives "at the wrong moment: too hot, too cold, the opera, theater, museum, is closed for the day, the season, or indefinitely for repairs, or else there is a strike, or an epidemic, or tanks are taking part in a political coup." None of that for the tourist, who is purchasing what one attractive brochure guarantees, "Absolute Peace of Mind."

A signal characteristic of the tourist is what Walker Percy calls "busy disregard"—that is, not experiencing the foreign moment at all because of being busy with camera, lenses, and film, or worried about tipping, or embarrassed over one's monolingualism, or deploring the state of local sanitation. Tourism invites, or rather, requires, an obsession with things that are not travel—the mechanics, rather than the objects and sensations, of displacement: the waiters and concierges, the currency exchanges and the swindles, the pickpockets, the hotels and meals, the value of purchasable things, the offensiveness or charm of one's fellows in the group. "Making new friends is one of the joys of travel," chirps Caravan Tours. "With Caravan, you'll find congenial companions of all ages. . . . You'll feel right at home."

Easy irony there, to be sure, but there are ironies everywhere in the world touristically conceived. Even Eugene Fodor, whose guidebooks have been among the most effective stimulators of international tourism, is now almost contrite about the damage he has wrought. In his guidebook *Rome, 1986,* he recognizes ruefully that as a result in part of his own efforts, 11,000 tourists per day now swamp the Sistine Chapel, making a visit to it "an equal blend of pleasure and torture." That precisely illustrates Patrick Leigh Fermor's point about tourism killing the thing it loves and may even suggest that when tourism becomes hellish enough, it will somehow come full circle and turn into something like travel again.

Another characteristic of tourism isn't mentioned much in public because it's politically a bit embarrassing. That is that tourism is a flagrantly reactionary activity. It's a way residents of the Free World go to patronize the poor. Except for wearing funny hats and being crisscrossed with camera straps and conglobulating in a close mass, a group of tourists politically resembles a collective British milord of the nineteenth century. Tourists behold the foreign destitute, scrutinize their rags and note their terrible food, observe their ramshackle dwellings and acquaint themselves with their ignorance and superstition, not with outrage or even pity, but with satisfaction. This "foreignness" is, after all, what the tourists have paid for, and their contract provides that it will keep its distance. We can call the unfortunates tourists pay to go look at *touristees*—South Sea islanders, the lifetime junk-dwellers of Hong Kong, the villagers of India, the young women of China who spend their lives making tiny stitches on horrible embroidered pictures to sell to tourists. *Touristees* are the geeks of the contemporary world, even if they don't eat live chickens for the amusement of their betters. This looking at the luckless without any impulse to alleviate their condition is clearly one of the most powerful signals of the reactionary attitude. Whatever their initial state, touristees are inevitably demeaned by tourism into the psychological and political inferiors of the tourists who view them—with the possible exception of the touristees who dwell in Paris and other sophisticated metropolises. Once out in the countryside, even in the gondolas of Venice, the horse carriages of Spétsai, or the bicycle rickshaws of Katmandu, no tourist can avoid condescending to his visible inferiors. Out of this comfortable insulation from misery grows the tourist conviction, indispensable if the whole operation is to work, that the deprived are really quite happy.

But when all this has been said, when we have taken the standard pleasure in damning tourists, we may have to acknowledge that maybe Culler is right when he points out that "The attempt to distinguish between tourists and travelers is a part of tourism—integral to it rather than outside or beyond it." As he says, "Part of what is involved in being a tourist is disliking tourists (both other tourists and the fact that one is a tourist)." The tourists on Swan's Hellenic Tours, visiting the Mediterranean and Aegean on their own elegant small liner accompanied by learned archaeological lecturers from Oxford and Cambridge, sneer at the other tourists being conveyed to the same sites by more plebeian transport and harangued not by distinguished authorities but by mere local guides. And those tourists in turn view with pity and contempt others gaping at the same sites from more derelict vehicles and listening to the explanation not of a guide but of a driver. And so it goes.

Again, one's complacency in damning tourists may receive a slight embarrassment by recalling one's own youth and recognizing that virtually everyone, no matter how would-be sophisticated ultimately, starts traveling as a tourist. One must, simply, experience the great things: Santa Sophia, the Piazza San Marco, Carcassonne and Chartres and Mont St. Michel, Red Square, Persepolis, Westminster Abbey, the Taj Mahal. These constitute the current Wonders of the World, and not to see them, tourist clichés as they may be, is to be forever deficient in the knowledge of what a Wonder is.

At any given moment, millions of tourists and several travelers are moving over the face of the globe, and one must ask what good, and what kind of good, results. Clearly this activity makes a lot of money for somebody, but what else? Is intelligence forwarded? Is virtue? Does any beneficial "international understanding" ensue? Dean MacCannell thinks so. He holds that one source of international social coherence is the very universal popularity of the standard touristic attractions. He argues that in the absence of any very compelling single system of ethical, political, or artistic agreement, in an age of relativism where argument about essentials is the norm and "deconstructive" doubts about stable values are commonplace, tourism has at least the merit of providing one area of substantial agreement—about "what is worth seeing." In Paris, the Japanese, the Germans, the Argentinians, and the Australians share at least one common belief, that it's important not to miss the Louvre. I suppose the young people who converge every spring and summer on the Acropolis or at the Spanish Steps or in the center of Picadilly Circus are too poor to be tourists and are thus, willy-nilly, travelers. But regardless, to overhear the babble of their idioms, in Hungarian, Portuguese, German, Swedish, French, Italian, American, and what-have-you, is to be persuaded that some sort of "international understanding," whatever that may mean, is taking place, and that what's taking place, no matter how hard to define, is an invaluable thing.

In trying to winkle some sense out of the notion of international understanding, we may perceive that *understanding* can betoken at least three quite different things. First, there is sentimental or social understanding, as when we note that someone is very understanding—that is, uncritical, sympathetic, and nice. That clearly is not the sort of understanding that results from wandering amidst the foreign. Nor is the second meaning of *understanding* very useful in gauging the benefits of travel. This second meaning takes *understanding* in a commercial or utilitarian sense, the sort of goal encouraged by the Business Council for International Understanding in Washington, D.C. Utilitarian understanding requires a businessman or international traveling salesman to know enough about the social customs of a foreign place not to jeopardize a deal by ignorance or clumsiness. Some of the dimensions of this kind of understanding are suggested by Roger T. Axtell's recent *Do's and Taboos Around the World: A Guide to International Behavior.* From this text the anxious businessman will learn that in most of Southeast Asia, as well as in the Middle East, presenting your business card with your left hand is an affront, every decent Moslem knowing the filthy, smelly offices you reserve that left hand for. But from Axtell's book you will learn also that in Japan, you must present your card with both hands, bowing while doing so and in addition making sure the card is right side up with the type readable by the recipient. Everywhere abroad the businessman must be very careful with gestures. Making a circle with thumb and forefinger, the way the President does every time he survives surgery, may mean "OK!" in the United States, but in Brazil it's grossly obscene, while in Japan it signifies "Money!" and in France, "Zero." Gifts of flowers can be risky too. In Belgium, for example, avoid bouquets of chrysanthemums, which the locals associate with death. In Mexico, yellow flowers of any kind suggest death. In Italy it's important that a bouquet contain an odd number of flowers—but in no instance thirteen. All these are of course useful tips which may augment one's business success and earning power. But not one's understanding, not, at least, in the honorific sense of that term.

These forms of sentimental and utilitarian understanding are to be distinguished from liberal understanding, where *liberal* has the same by now hackneyed meaning it has in the phrase liberal arts. The liberal principle of disinterested or nonutilitarian perception and contemplation is now as often honored in public as ignored in private. Motivated purely by curiosity, you pursue liberal understanding neither to be nice to people nor to put money in your pocket but to glorify your human nature and to augment your awareness of your location in time and space. You pursue liberal understanding to deepen your sensitivity to ideas and images and not least to sharpen your sense of humility as you come to realize that your country is not the "standard" for the rest of the world but is just as odd as all the others. As Flaubert observes, "Traveling makes one modest. You see what a tiny place you occupy in the world."

Anyone teased by the question, How to regain the values of travel in an age of mass tourism, might consider a fairly bold and simple answer. You regain them the way you might regain real education in a contemporary context of business, law, and medical schools—namely, by stimulating the impulse of disinterested intellectual curiosity, the habit of inquiry for its own sake. (It's remarkable and alarming the way the concept *graduate school,* which used to suggest study toward the Ph.D. degree in some civilizing subject, now connotes to most Americans the place where you earn your M.B.A.) Recovering real education, as opposed to training, would not be easy to do. It would be just as hard as recovering real travel, but the two things are so nearly allied as to constitute two faces of the same thing, and the absence of one is a clear sign of the absence of the other. In celebrating genuine travel, Robert Byron comes close to defining the unchanging spirit of liberal learning. He writes:

> For some persons there exists an organic harmony between all matter and all activity, whose discovery is the purpose of their lives and whose evidence, being inexhaustible, can only be selected by the good judgment and perpetual curiosity of the individual. . . . These persons are the traveling species. The *pleasures* of travel need no reiteration. But when the impulse is so imperious that it amounts to a spiritual necessity, then travel must rank with the more serious form of endeavor. Admittedly there are other ways of making the world's acquaintance. But the traveler is a slave to his senses; his grasp of a fact can only be complete when reinforced by sensory evidence; he can know the world, in fact, only when he sees, hears, and smells it. Hence [the traveler's] craving for personal reconnaissance. . . .

And unlike the sentimental "understander," the liberal traveler—the phrase is really redundant—does not expect his personal reconnaissance to result always in optimistic news. That is, you don't have to like a place to understand it, or, to put it another way, life is not a vacation. Indeed, liberal understanding is entirely consistent with the sort of perception resulting in a statement like "You really have to understand the Swiss [Greeks, Turks, Iranians, Indians, etc.] to despise them."

What you understand by traveling depends, clearly, on

where you start and what you begin with. A Pakistani will understand something very different from traveling in, say, southern France than a resident of New Jersey. But narrowing the focus to an American traveling in Europe—really traveling, not being insulated from actuality—one can ask, what is he or she likely to "understand"? First of all, the North American will not be abroad very long without beginning to understand that the U.S. "friendly" style is not international. It's not even, as the naïve might think, "normal" or "natural," and thus happy evidence of the absence of a possibly disingenuous personal style: it *is* a style, just like any other, and abroad, the American will learn, it is not just odd but offensive. Non-Americans have mastered the paradox that it is formality rather than informality that lubricates social encounters. Thus in France *monsieur* and *madame,* in Italy *dottore* and *avvocato.*

And an American's understanding of international reality would deepen as he or she began to penetrate beneath matters of address and etiquette. The American abroad would begin to understand that the world outside the United States is deeply aware, as we are not, of the past. Here, the idea suggests at most a late-seventeenth-century stockade (restored) at Jamestown or the pretty, benign buildings of the restored Williamsburg. Abroad, on the other hand, the American will come into repeated contact with a past much deeper than that and much less gratifying in its implicit news about the beneficence of human impulses. He will confront a plethora of ancient, medieval, and Renaissance castles and fortified places organized for little but defense against gross physical violence. The traveler, and even the tourist, will behold things quite unknown in the United States, where the Disney version of life aspires to replace the traditional one. He will behold city walls everywhere and churches and cathedrals with massive metal-studded doors and moats and portcullises and drawbridges and buildings with no windows lower than the fourth story. Observing these relics of some mighty unpleasant facts, the traveler will come to understand that violence and cruelty and sadism, and defenses against these things, have shaped European and Asian "politics" for millennia. By means of Robert Byron's "personal reconnaissance," the traveler will perceive that most of the world outside the very singular United States lives always with vivid memories of physical coercion, torture for the fun of it, and meaningless violent death. No wonder people abroad seem to many Americans models of "pessimism," "cynicism," or at least "irony." For us, whose past does not extend further back than the optimistic and relatively civilized eighteenth century, the foreign past is a shocking panorama of religious mass murders, drawings and quarterings, burnings at the stake, invasions, aerial bombings, piracies, and such un-American events (at least since our destruction of the American indigenes) as the massacre of the Armenians, the liquidation of the kulaks, and the Holocaust. In his recent suggestively titled book *Painted in Blood: Understanding Europeans,* Stuart Miller notes "the deep imprint of organized horror on the European soul," which means that abroad the air is alive with tragedy and its inevitable accompaniment, irony. Even without the specifically tragic sense of human evil in action, living among the quite inert ruins of the Forum, the Great Wall, the Pyramids, or Mycenae must encourage the ironic view of one's own little concerns, and you can't help seeing in your mind's eye your own precious setting ruined in due course and then visited by hordes of uncomprehending tourists with their keepers, avid for a sit-down and a nice cold Coca-Cola. As Stuart Miller puts it,

> To be an American is to live next to man-made things, most of which are no older than you are. [Thus,] the impression that the world began about the time you did . . . reinforces the illusion that your mastery over exis-tence is potentially without limits, almost infinite. . . . [In Europe] the daily evidence of the past reminds you often of the transitory, if not tragic character of human exis-tence.

In the United States, if you want to sense the ironic relation between past and present, you read *The Waste Land* or *Ulysses*. Abroad, you raise your eyes from your book and look around.

But speaking of "the past," the experience I've been talking about may seem already archaic—not just that it's been displaced by a cheerful, superficial tourism but that tourism itself has been overtaken by something new. We can call it *post-tourism*. That term would designate a stage in the history of traveling characterized by boredom, annoyance, disgust, disillusion, and finally anger. The most recent travvelers seem to travel no longer to experience the historical irony that "modernism" brought to our notice. Rather, they seem en-meshed in the "postmodern" refusal to take seriously the pretenses of traditional ethical historiography or of the recent intellectual world. These new travelers seem to doubt that the world available for scrutiny is a place where any stable understanding, interpretation, or even enjoyment is likely.

Without straining for the parallel, one can see the post-touristic style in perception and articulation as a corollary of "deconstruction" in contemporary literary theory. In both there is a similar impatience with the perceptual techniques or certainties of the past, a similar conviction that such former values as unity, coherence, continuity, moral stability, and unalterable meaning are now obsolete. A similar skepticism about deriving meaningful humanistic instruction from either physical settings or literary texts seems to mark both post-touristic travel and deconstruction. Both recoil with some contempt and disgust from the pretensions of the contemporary world to deliver value and meaning, let alone the former hoped-for dividend of both travel and literature, "wisdom."

Now, somehow, the bloom is off both activities, and a term like "understanding" acquires overtones of quaintness. Or so one might infer from a number of current travel books, fit to be subtitled, like John Krich's account of his Asian travels in 1984, *Around the World in a Bad Mood.* (His thoroughly depressing title is *Music in Every Room,* a quote from a handbill advertising a horrible mock-Western hotel in India.) As an epigraph for his book Krich has chosen a passage from Lévi-Strauss's *Tristes Tropiques,* a work which more than any other has helped establish the intellectual and emotional style of post-tourism. Published in 1955 (roughly the moment when jet travel began replacing former kinds), Lévi-Strauss opens with a chapter beginning "I hate travelers and explorers," and he goes on to argue the virtual impossibility of "understanding" anything about other people by "travel" among them in the old sense. As the equally skeptical John Krich says about *Tristes Tropiques,*

> It was a book set in Brazil that told us the most about what we could, or couldn't see in Asia. Claude Lévi-Strauss turned out to be our most articulate ally, whose respect for the savage was tempered by his weariness at ever understanding him, or himself. *Tristes Tropiques* became our true guidebook. . . .

And Krich shares Lévi-Strauss's conviction that modern industrialism has so ruined the world that no place can be any longer a refuge from pollution, corruption, and Western-style commercialism. Thus "trying to escape—at least in ways that travel brochures promise—is like trying to escape death. We know that we can't really do it, but that all the meaning we'll ever find will be in the effort." Some meaning can be found too, by the posttourist, in the exercise of noting unpleasant facts and registering them in the kind of brutally honest formulations tourism cannot stand. For example, Krich particularly likes an Australian couple he meets, finding them appealing "because they were so willing to whine about Asian conditions and Asian pretensions."

Similarly, one British travel journalist, Digby Anderson, has recently recommended a new kind of "negative" touristic writing designed to discourage tourists from going to certain places by the unaccustomed act of telling the truth. The object of such negative travel writing, he says, is "to make readers think twice before going, to protect them from the temptations of . . . [travel] agents, to undermine rather than inflate their self-confidence, indeed to reduce those going to that minimum which will really enjoy it." He proposes some sample sentences from such writings, like: "All the French Mediterranean is horrid in August. Don't go," and "Taormina may have been pleasant once; it isn't now." The same writer has suggested that travel consumers should be informed seriously that travel is like liberal learning, difficult if worth having. Travel writers, he insists, "need to remind us that pleasure demands effort and is improved by knowledge and taste." He goes on: "It is unusual . . . to deny this about literature, music, or painting. Why should it be any less true of travel and holiday?"

Telling the awful truth about places is distinctly one of the gestures of post-tourism. Patrick White, traveling in Greece, sounds the true note:

Gythion turned out a somewhat unprepossessing town, with . . . some of the worst plumbing and food. There is a small island, Crainai, where Paris and Helen are said to have enjoyed each other after their elopement. Today the island is linked to the town by a causeway, . . . the Mecca of German hippies with camper vans. It was littered with rubbish and human shit. Still, we enjoyed climbing the terraces of Gythion, asking directions and general information of friendly women, and sipping our

ouzo in a cool breeze beside a sea which smelled un-
avoidably of sewage.

There, the pleasant details—Paris and Helen, the nice
women—seem present only to underscore the nastiness.
And as Paul Theroux, one undoubted master of the post-
touristic mode, walks around the British coast, he does so
with a powerful elegiac understanding that its former attractiveness is gone forever:

> The rock pools of Devon and Cornwall had been vio-
> lated, and Dunwich had sunk into the sea, and Prestatyn
> was littered, and Sunderland was unemployed. Oddest
> of all, there were hardly any ships on a coast that had
> once been crammed with them. "Once a great port," the
> guidebook always said of the seaside towns.

With Theroux, it's hard not to notice how often he enjoys
the awfulness he's experiencing, with what pleasure he confirms his worst suspicions about the badness of airlines,
trains, hotels, guides, and famous places. Anatole Broyard
would seem to have Theroux in mind (although he could just
as easily be thinking of V. S. Naipaul or Philip Glazebrook or
William Golding) when he points out how many current
travelers "take a positive delight in awfulness." Observing
Belfast, Theroux says, "It was so awful, I wanted to stay." If
"it really was one of the nastiest cities in the world, surely
then it was worth spending some time in, for horror interest?" For these new post-touristic observers, Broyard contin-

ues, awfulness is "the contemporary equivalent of the exotic"
—which used to be the magnet for their traveling predecessors. The essay in which Broyard delivers these accurate
perceptions is nicely titled, "Having Minimalist Time, Wish
You Were Here."

If universal litter and filth are one cause of post-touristic dismay, another is the homogenization of the modern
world, the spread into even the most unlikely places of the
uniform airport and hotel and frozen "international" food
and standard "travel agency." Prophesying about the 1960s,
Evelyn Waugh, in an essay titled "I See Nothing but Boredom Everywhere," observed that genuine foreign travel
would become one of the main casualties. Formerly, he says,
"One went abroad to observe other ways of living, to eat
unfamiliar foods and see strange buildings." But soon, he
notes prophetically, the world will be divided into, on the
one hand, "zones of insecurity" dominated by terrorism and,
on the other, flashy and vulgar tourist sites where one will
be conveyed by the uniform jet to "chain hotels, hygienic,
costly, and second-rate."

Although now almost impossible to believe, air travel
was once civilized and pleasant. On a flight in the 1930s,
Paul Bowles recalls, "I had my own cabin with a bed in it,
and under sheet and blankets I slept during most of the
flight." And equally hard to believe: in 1944 Charles A.
Lindbergh flew TWA from San Francisco to New York and
noted that "an excellent meal is served on all these domestic
airlines." But forty years later the progress of the tourist
industry had brought many more people than travel-smarties
to a full post-touristic attitude. "I realized with a shock,"

Bowles says now, "that not only did the world have many more people in it than it had a short time before, but also that the hotels were less good, travel less comfortable, and places in general much less beautiful. . . . I realized to what an extent the world had worsened." His conclusion, mistaken as some may think it, will strike others as the only honest one for a person of knowledge, sensibility, and taste: "I no longer wanted to travel."

Whether one shares it or not, the post-touristic approach is at least a useful reminder that you don't have to admire, or even like, a place to "understand" it. Those who know Calcutta, Manila, Haiti, and what Theroux calls "the horror cities of Northern England" will get the point. Hilary Mantel, a young British traveler, recalls her experience of this principle, and in doing so suggests her passage from the uncritical acceptances of tourism to the skepticisms of post-tourism:

When I traveled at first I used to ask what I could get out of it, and what I could give back. What could I teach, and what could I learn? I saw the world as some sort of exchange scheme for my ideals, but the world deserves better than this. When you come across an alien culture you must not automatically respect it. You must sometimes pay it the compliment of hating it.

Thus Theroux could be said to "understand" the Republic of India when he's revolted by the daily spectacle of middle-class Indians excreting all along the railway tracks. "At first," he says, "I thought they were simply squatting comfortably to watch the train go by." All were "facing the train for the diversion it offered, unhurriedly fouling the track." That suggests that real international understanding is entirely compatible with disgust, which can be as salutary and instructive as approval.

Consider the experience of Robert Byron in the Soviet Union in 1932. He found himself appalled by the cost that mechanical Leninism seemed to exact in art, in taste, in ideas, in general subtlety, and in simple human honesty, not to mention "international understanding." Moving about the U.S.S.R. and being constantly adjured to admire the glories of communism, he noted "the pleasant feeling of pugnacity that awoke in my bosom." The instructive yield of the whole painful experience wasn't clear until he returned home and found that the yardstick provided by Soviet awfulness could measure the inestimable value of what before he had been rather inclined to take for granted. One's disgust with the Soviet shackling of thought, he found, "Washes away the layers of complacence that accumulate through residence in the civilized—perhaps too civilized—capitals of the West. At the same time it stirs a new and combative faith in the ultimate future of Western civilization and a resolution never to sacrifice individual integrity of thought."

The true disinterestedness of the genuine traveler may seem more self-indulgent and perhaps even socially irresponsible today than ever before, in the current atmosphere of "assured nuclear destruction." Some may fear that open expressions of international detestation may risk igniting the terrible fuse. But to withhold criticism for that reason would be both sentimentally to overestimate real national sensitivities (as opposed to national publicity mechanisms) and to underestimate the absolute necessity of, as Matthew Arnold put it, "the free play of the mind on all subjects, for its own sake." If we think of the mind as a sensorium in motion, kinetic, not static, impelled by curiosity to drain meaning from strange place after strange place, "the free play of the mind on all subjects, for its own sake" is as good an indication of what genuine travel involves as we're likely to come across. And despite tourism and post-tourism (and deconstruction), meaning is there to be found—so long as the mind is really free.

ON THE
PERSISTENCE
OF
PASTORAL

A topic not much speculated about these days is the origin, perhaps even the psychological foundation, of the system of literary—largely "poetic"—genres that dominated Western writing during antiquity and the Renaissance. Where do they come from, these conventional thematic forms? Why does their number seem limited? And what explains their acceptability and persistence? I am not talking about such large modes as narrative, lyric, and dramatic, which differ from genres in constituting different essential ways of delivering imaginative material. The distinctions there are between radicals, as Northrop Frye has put it, of presentation and address, the degree to which the utterer dramatizes his voice or devises voices for other people. I am talking about such conventional genres as tragedy, epic, elegy, epitaph, epigram, epistle, song, ode, satire, and, the topic here, pastoral. I have listed ten of these genres: why would it be difficult to add an eleventh? Why does the number seem finite?

Alexander Pope lived in the age of Linnaeus, an age adept at analysis and fascinated by the act of classification. That Bible of the age, John Locke's *Essay Concerning Human Understanding,* specifically warns against equating or confusing two things that are merely similar but never identical. When Pope thought about writing, which he seems to have done constantly, he was likely to do so by means of the technique of analysis and differentiation, and to recur to the traditional system of genres. In the collection of his poems which he issued in 1717, he was careful to arrange the items in such a way as to make the volume a virtual display cabinet of the genres, exhibiting his skill in things as different as the Pindaric Ode and the Ovidian Heroic Epistle. The origins of the genres was a topic Pope was not averse to ruminating about, and on one occasion, interested in the prehistorical folk origins of ode and its obverse, satire—that is, the poem of praise and the poem of dispraise—he arrived at some insights (or at least images) useful to anyone who wants to think about this subject.

The occasion was his "imitation" of the First Epistle of the Second Book of Horace, a poem about patronage, literary theory, and literary history which he addressed "To Augustus"—meaning, ironically and satirically, George III, conspicuous as an ignorer of the arts if not an active traducer of them. In this poem Pope, like Horace before him, is at pains to establish an acceptable moral provenance for the genre *satire*. His task is to argue that satire can be traced to an understandable psychological and social origin, an origin sanctified by its location among "the folk," or, as Pope terms them, "Our rural ancestors," presumably of the Neolithic Age. Among their most treasured annual holidays was Harvest Home, the day the grain was all brought in. It was devoted to feasting, drinking, and merrymaking, thanksgiving, and even sacrificing:

> Our rural ancestors, with little blest,
> Patient of labor when the end was rest,
> Indulged the day that housed their annual grain
> With feasts, and off'rings, and a thankful strain.

No one was excluded from the celebration:

> The joy their wives, their sons, and servants share,
> Ease of their toil, and partners of their care.

The drinking at first produced only levity:

> The laugh, the jest, attendants on the bowl,
> Smoothed every brow, and opened every soul.

But as the custom was repeated century after century, the jests formalized into the tradition of *flyting:*

> With growing years the pleasing license grew,
> And taunts alternate innocently flew.

And these "taunts alternate" gradually turned more drunken and brutal, until the insults, remembered all year long, began to poison civil life:

> But times corrupt, and nature, ill-inclined,
> Produced the point that left a sting behind,
> Till friend with friend, and families at strife,
> Triumphant malice raged through private life.

Those most grievously libeled had recourse to law, which wisely prescribed limits to insult. The limits, we are to understand, evolved into artistic conventions allowing satire to be identified as a form of art distinguished from mere crude abuse. "At length," Pope goes on,

> by wholesome dread of statutes bound,
> The poets learned to please, and not to wound.

Some poets hoped to avoid trouble entirely by turning satire inside out and writing its reverse, the ode; or, as Pope puts it,

Most warped to flattery's side.

But some, he says, were capable of finer distinctions. They stayed with satire but refined it:

> some, more nice,
> Preserved the freedom and forebore the vice.

The result was a genre that cunningly blends rude abuse and fine art, known to the Ancients as well as the Moderns:

> Hence satire rose, that just the medium hit,
> And heals with morals what it hurts with wit.

Pope's aim, of course, is to justify satire, to clear it of charges of lawlessness. A genre like pastoral requires no such justification. In Pope's day theory of the pastoral poem was entangled in the question whether Theocritus or Virgil provided the best model. That is, whether one's pastorals should be blunt and low-down, like those of Ambrose Phillips, or suave and elevated, like those of Pope himself. But when a critic like Pope attends to questions of the origin of pastoral, he finds that pastorals were originally poems sung by shepherds themselves celebrating "their own felicity." And that later, more corrupt and sophisticated ages used the form to project "a perfect image" of "that happy time," the Golden Age of innocence. That is, literate ages have used the pastoral genre in large part as a compensatory device, a way of vacationing from actuality. The tradition, all the way from Edmund Spenser in the sixteenth century to Matthew Arnold in the nineteenth, provides a way of realizing conventionally an alternative to the experiential world. Milton's Eden in *Paradise Lost* is a near-classic version of traditional pastoral, even if Adam and Eve tend a garden instead of a flock, because it so fully establishes an ideal for physical nature, wishing it back into its state before the Fall. Pastoral depicts the Other. It exhibits what we would have *if only*. If only people were simple and generous. If only they hadn't chosen to live in cities and pursue greedy commercial goals. As Renato Poggioli notes in *The Oaten Flute,* "The poetry of the pastoral embraces both longing and wish fulfillment. As a consequence, the definition of poetry that Bacon gives in *The Advancement of Learning* is particularly well suited to the pastoral, since this poetic form succeeds even better than others in 'submitting the shows of things to the desires of the mind.'"

Thus the origin of the poetic genres in certain universal psychological needs. The need to contemplate heroes is satisfied by epic, while the need to understand the decisions of heroes as ironic prompts the creation of tragedy. Elegy is the form devised for the recurring human need to utter valediction, and epitaph is its "operational" cemetery sibling. Epigram takes care of the need to be witty, the experience of joy in thought. Epistle recognizes the urge to communicate with distant friends. Song is where one places the sheer irresponsible feeling of happiness, occasioned by love or drink, when it occurs. Ode is the receptacle for the impulse to honor and praise, satire the vehicle for the opposite impulse, the urge to denigrate. Notable in this system of genres is a certain symmetry, or even what we can call emotional counterpoise. If ode is balanced by satire, then the epic or heroic is balanced by pastoral, which, like these others, corresponds to one of the finite, universal impulses—the urge to escape the actual to lodge in something closer to the ideal.

In late-industrial society this generic system attenuates, or, to use again the terminology of Northrop Frye, "displaces." But it doesn't really disappear, the emotional needs on which it is based being lodged so deeply in the human psyche. These essential human emotional needs and the genres which correspond to them are what thinkers of Pope's age called Nature, that is, essential human nature, unchanging and always visible despite temporary alterations in form and style. To take as an example only pastoral, it seems part of its character that like matter, the pastoral impulse—that is, the hankering after an easier form of the world—is never destroyed. Founded as it is on the bedrock of universal human wishes, it merely changes its external shape from age to age, incarnating itself now in this form, now in that, but never vanishing. "The pastoral fallacy and its equivalents," Poggioli reminds us, "are deeply rooted in human nature; this explains the recurrence or permanence of their manifestations and the survival of pastoral make-believe even in such an Iron Age as ours."

Looking hastily at the contemporary scene, one might easily conceive that pastoral had disappeared. And those who assume that human nature alters dramatically over the course of history and that it alters always in a "progressive" way do so conceive, finding pastoral as outmoded as knee breeches and farthingales. Thus John Barrell and John Bull, editors of *The Penguin Book of English Pastoral Verse.* Believing that society is gradually but inexorably improving, they find that "as the possibility of social mobility and of economic progress increases, so the pastoral tradition, which had originally rested on a separation of social worlds, is first threatened and finally almost fades away." By identifying pastoral too literally and rigidly with the form it took when the term betokened poems involving shepherds, Barrell and Bull are easily convinced that the tradition is unlikely to survive our time. What they have missed is that poems depicting shepherds constitute only one incarnation of an impulse which is permanent and unchangeable. It would be a grave understatement to point out that much has changed since the sixteenth century and that the changes have been most conspicuous in political and social arrangements, as critics of a Marxist tendency like Barrell and Bull emphasize, and in technology. But an observer with perhaps a firmer grip on the whole history of emotion and imagery, the British poet David Jones, concludes otherwise.

His long poem of 1937, *In Parenthesis,* seeks to attach deep historical resonances to the trench warfare of the First World War. Thus his British soldiers "recall" earlier service with the Roman legions, and when they are killed at Mametz Wood, a forest spirit from ancient European folklore, the Queen of the Woods, offers them solace by presenting flowers to their dead bodies. Readers differ about Jones's success in treating the horrors of that war in this highly self-conscious, overwhelmingly allusive way. But they would probably agree that given Jones's Christian insistence that human nature has changed little since antiquity, his method is, logically, appropriate. His view of human nature as largely unchanging he presents in his preface, where, although he admits that "our culture has accelerated every line of advance into the territory of physical science," he still notices that underneath we are the same old people. He goes to certain central human actions as illustrations: "We stroke cats, pluck flowers, tie ribands, assist at the manual arts of religion, make some kind of love, write poems, paint pictures, are generally at one with the creaturely world inherited from our remote beginnings." It is to the finite emotional actions of that pre-literary "creaturely world" that we must trace the origins of the literary genres of antiquity.

David Jones is only one of many who fought the First World War comforted by memories of pastoral poetry and alert for opportunities to take refuge in what Poggioli has termed "pastoral oases"—in his sense, moments of relaxation and refreshment observable in late-medieval and Renaissance European narratives. For the troops of the Great War, "pastoral oases" were less literary than actual—moments of safety behind the line, leaves at home, recuperative stays in hospital. The imaginative behavior of these soldiers indicates that the opposite of experiencing moments of war is proposing moments of pastoral. Pastoral—if no longer the poetry, then the body of imagery and emotion associated with it—provides the model world by which the demonism of warfare is measured.

It has been said that what makes the world so hard to understand is that there's nothing to compare it with. But that's not right: there's literature to compare it with—

especially pastoral, conceived as an activity ranging from evanescent daydream to formal, public literary registration.

For the British soldiers confined to the trenches of the First World War, imaginative recourse to pastoral details was a popular way to protect oneself against horror and fear. Among these soldiers, the Arcadian Golden Age posited by Classical and Renaissance poetic pastoral—that place and time of innocence and pleasure—finds its "displaced" counterpart in place-images of "home" and time-images of the prewar "summer of 1914." Bucolic details become a significant standard of measurement in Wilfred Owen's poem "Exposure." The scene is the very severe winter of 1917. Owen depicts himself and his freezing companions huddling in forward holes during a blizzard:

> Pale flakes with fingering stealth come feeling for our
>   faces,
> We cringe in holes, back on forgotten dreams, and
>   stare, snow-dazed,
> Deep into grassier ditches. So we drowse,
>   sun-dozed,
> Littered with blossoms trickling where the blackbird
>   fusses.
>   Is it that we are dying?

Presented with the datum *snow-dazed,* the imagination remembers the ideal pastoral and from it supplies a gauge: *sun-dozed.*

That is a pastoral oasis triggered by a slant rhyme.

Here's another pastoral refuge of a different kind. Noting how rarely one caught sight of the enemy across No Man's Land, the British memorist Guy Chapman recalls that

> Once we heard him. On a morning when light filtered through a bleached world, and a blanket of mist was spread upon the ground so that our eyes could only pierce to the edge of our own wire, the whole company seized the opportunity to repair the damages of shell fire. We worked furiously with muffled mauls and all the coils of wire we could beg. Presently we realized that the enemy was doing as we were; dull thuds and the chink and wrench of wire came from his side. We might perhaps have opened fire, but that suddenly there came out of the blankness the sound of a young voice.

And as he goes on, Chapman seems to remember the term Dorian in a special way, the way the pastoral context of Matthew Arnold's *Thyrsis* gives that word a meaning synonymous with Doric—that is, attractively rustic, pastoral. The young voice sounding through the mist, says Chapman,

> was raised in some Dorian-mooded folksong. High and high it rose, echoing and filling the mist, pure, too pure for this draggled hill-side. We stopped our work to listen. No one would have dared to break the fragile echo. As we listened, the fog shifted a little, swayed and began to melt. We collected our tools and bundled back to our

trench. The singing voice drew further off, as if it was only an emanation of the drifting void.

Chapman's description of the "Dorian-mooded" song as "pure, too pure for this draggled hill-side" registers his sense that what he is hearing is "the other," the ideal, the never realized in the fallen world—here, displaced pastoral.

But useful as pastoral consciousness is for purposes of refuge or comfort, it serves yet another function on the Western Front. It assists ironic perception of one's absurd, murderous predicament there. As David Kalstone once observed, even when it has been regarded ironically, "a clarifying or restorative force . . . has always been associated with pastoral." The First World War ironist is thus able, if not to have it both ways, at least to involve himself in a fructive ambiguity. By drawing upon pastoral details, he can measure the distance between the actual and the desirable and at the same time create a small oasis for his brief occupancy, as Wilfred Owen does in his well-known sonnet "Anthem for Doomed Youth." There, the detail of

The shrill, demented choirs of wailing shells

both gauges the obscenity of industrialized murder and returns speaker and listener for a fleeting moment to the pastoral world where "choirs" consist of benign insects and birds.

But strictly speaking, pastoral requires shepherds and their sheep, and the young British officers who led troops in the First World War very often had recourse to pastoral images as they contemplated their responsibilities. Troop leaders as well as the clergy automatically become *pastors* to C. E. Montague, who writes in *Disenchantment* of the newly volunteered troops' rapid passage from enthusiasm to cynicism. "In the first weeks of the war," he says, "most of the flock had too simply taken on trust all that its pastors and masters had said." Later they discovered that "in the lump pastors and masters were frauds." Milton's *Lycidas* seems to be Montague's reference point: the title of his chapter about the defects of military chaplains and the sad insufficiency of the official religious consolations is "The Sheep That Were Not Fed." When a body of men in training is marched by its sergeant directly to a public house with whose landlord he has an understanding, the moralists who decline to enter and who stand around outside all afternoon finally begin to break down into cynicism and to wonder, in the words of *Lycidas,* "Were it not better done as others use?"

Actually, there seems no action or emotion of the front line during the First World War that cannot be accommodated to some part of the pastoral paradigm. In his poem "Going into the Line," the writer with the quintessentially English name of Max Plowman contrives to dominate the bombardment by imagining an almost literal pastoral oasis:

And slowly in his overheated mind
Peace like a river through a desert flows,
And sweetness wells and overflows in streams
That reach the farthest friend in memory.

Now that he has quieted himself by fantasizing this scene, he can contemplate his relation to the men he is commanding, and he finds that he feels a silent, secret

> dear delight in serving these,
> These poor sheep, driven innocent to death.

Likewise, the birds and flowers associated with literary pastoral are invoked repeatedly by soldiers hoping to make some traditional sense of their experience in the trenches. One of the most remarkable of all intersections between life and literature occurred when the soldiers discovered that Flanders and Picardy abounded literally in the two kinds of birds long the property of purely ideal literary pastoral—larks and nightingales. The lark became associated with the dawn ceremony of stand-to in the trenches, the nightingale with stand-to at evening. Such a symmetrical arrangement was already available in Miltonic quasi-pastoral, where *L'Allegro* has its lark and *Il Penseroso* its nightingale. The soldiers imputed to these two species of birds meanings already attached to them by literary pastoral. The lark, heard first thing in the morning, betokened that one had got safely through another night and that perhaps, despite appearances, joy was still an active principle in the universe. And the nightingale provided a reminder of the sort of passionate beauty of which the war was the antithesis. Irony was the inevitable result of hearing it. Siegfried Sassoon remembered a nighttime moment, in spring 1918, near the Somme: "Nightingales were singing beautifully. . . . But the sky winked and glowed with swift flashes of the distant bombardments at Amiens and Albert, and there was a faint rumbling low and menacing. And still the nightingales sang on. O world God made!" A quarter of a century later, in the midst of another European war, an Allied soldier in Italy reveals further the persistence of these two pastoral birds. To British rifleman Alex Bowlby, the lark is still a token of ecstasy, and thus, when juxtaposed with the carnage, a trigger of irony. "In the lulls between explosions," says Bowlby, "I could hear a lark singing." That, he recalls, "made the war seem sillier than ever." Again, Bowlby, under fire from German self-propelled guns, hears bird song and thinks at first it may be the enemy signaling by means of birdcalls. "But as the bird sang on," he says, "I realized that no human could reproduce such perfection. It was a nightingale. And as if showing us and the Germans that there were better things to do it opened up until the whole valley rang with song. . . . I sensed a tremendous affirmation that [life] would go on."

In the same way that the birds of the front were selected for written registrations of experience there because they had already proved their usefulness in literary pastorals or quasi-pastorals, so with flowers. Despite the plethora of flowers visible on the Western Front—some way behind it, actually—in general two species only are singled out for notice: red roses and red poppies. Red flowers like these became fixtures of experience because they had already attained an indispensable place in pastoral elegy, where red or purple flowers, like "that sanguine flower inscrib'd with woe" of Milton's *Lycidas,* are traditional. (Red and purple, perhaps, because those are the colors of arterial and venous

blood. And the flowers are perennials, betokening resurrec-
tion.) Flanders fields are actually as profuse in bright blue
cornflowers as in scarlet poppies. But blue cornflowers, having no connection with pastoral elegiac convention, won't do
as funerary properties. In short, the "poppies" associated
with anniversaries of the Great War derive from pastoral
poetry and persist long after that poetry has formally van-
ished. The little paper poppies sold on the London streets
every November 11 derive originally from pastoral elegy.
They remind everyone of the dead of the First World War,
but they remind the literate especially of Milton's Arcadian
valleys which "purple all the ground with vernal flowers."
The way poppies as red pastoral flowers survive the formal
disappearance of pastoral poetry can be seen from one moment in *Sagittarius Rising,* a memoir by the First World War
aviator Cecil Lewis. He is walking over a bit of the now
largely disused Somme battlefield, observing its desolated,
riven trees, its debris and rubble everywhere, its overlapping
filthy shell craters extending to the horizon. "It was dis-
eased," says Lewis, "pocked, rancid, stinking of death in the
morning sun":

Yet (Oh, the catch at the heart!), among the devastated
cottages, the tumbled, twisted trees, the desecrated cem-
eteries, opening, candid, to the blue heaven, the poppies
were growing! Clumps of crimson poppies, thrusting out
from the lips of craters, struggling in drifts between the
hummocks, undaunted by the desolation, heedless of
human fury and stupidity, Flanders poppies, basking in
the sun.

And suddenly, "a lark rose up from among them and mounted, shrilling over the diapason of the guns."

Someone who would enjoy to the fullest an effect like that is Edmund Blunden, a notable figure in the persistence of pastoral. A lieutenant in the war, he recalled it in his subtle memoir *Undertones of War,* which resembles an extended pastoral elegy in prose. "Pastoral" surely is Blunden's view of the French countryside, once a verdant refuge, now brutally torn by bombardment: "The greensward, suited by nature for the raising of sheep, was all holes, and new ones appeared with great uproar as one passed." Blunden's investment in the pastoral paradigm is so deep that we suspect he is being literal when he populates the as yet unruined countryside west of the Somme with "naiads" and "hamadryads," destined to be destroyed, with their woods, in the German attack of March 1918. Compared with these timorous creatures, the nymphs of Milton's *Il Penseroso,* whose woodland haunts are threatened by the "rude axe," seem merely literary. It is always the innocence of nature conceived pastorally that Blunden emphasizes; in his understanding nature has not yet "fallen": it is the damage the war visits upon it which is its Fall. Observing the not yet ruined rural scene near Buire-sur-Ancre, he asks: "Could any countryside be more sweetly at rest, . . . more incapable of dreaming a field-gun? Fortunate it was that at the moment I was filled with this simple joy. . . . No conjecture that, in a few weeks, Buire-sur-Ancre [would be destroyed], came from that innocent greenwood." (We may feel as if *As You Like It* were written yesterday.) If such accomplished practitioners of English literary pastoral as Spenser or Milton or Thomas Gray or William Collins or Matthew Arnold had fought in the First World War, any one

of them could have used the image Blunden invokes to end
Undertones of War. Especially Milton, the Milton who so often
"pastoralizes" *Paradise Lost.* Noting the innocence with which
as a soldier youth he regarded the still undamaged countryside and aware of its ironic future, Blunden writes: "No
destined anguish lifted its snaky head to poison a harmless
young shepherd in a soldier's coat."

That brings us some distance from the idea of pastoral
understood by Theocritus, Virgil, Spenser, Milton, and Pope.
What we perceive now are survivals more thematic than
formal, or, strictly speaking, generic. Defining exactly these
surviving pastoral motifs is not easy, as Edward L. Ruhe
perceives. Finding what he calls "pastorality" in many films,
like *Days of Heaven,* he writes: "Pastorality may be taken as
an attribute of certain art works which it may seem eccentric
to nominate as pastorals." And he goes on:

> Pastoral is a "matter," like the old "matter of Troy" and
> the Arthurian legendry. Centrally, it has been the matter
> of the felicity of shepherds . . . ; and within pastorality
> the shepherd has been generalized to herdsman, to sim-
> ple rustic, to the folk, and in . . . radical displacements,
> to any simple being. . . . The term *pastoral* is so employed
> that we readily understand it to mean a thing, an attri-
> bute, a system of genres, a subject matter, and still more,
> depending on the context in which we find it.

"The shepherd has been generalized to herdsman," says
Ruhe. We can add that in *Lady Chatterley's Lover* D. H. Law-

rence displaces him to gamekeeper and in *A Farewell to Arms* Ernest Hemingway displaces him further to the Italian priest identified with the pastoral oasis of Abruzzi, the Italian place which, though cold, in the rainy, muddy atmosphere of War stands for an almost magical "other." Talking to Frederic Henry, in the midst of the sordid, noisy, obscene, cynical officers' mess, the priest says: "I would like you to go to Abruzzi. . . . There is good hunting. You would like the people and though it is cold it is clear and dry. You could stay with my family." And as Frederic imagines the place, he fills in details drawn from Ruhe's "pastorality": in Abruzzi, he conceives, "the roads were frozen and hard as iron, . . . it was clear cold and dry and the snow was dry and powdery and hare-tracks in the snow and the peasants took off their hats and called you Lord and there was good hunting."

Like the Italian priest is another Hemingway character resonant with pastorality, Bill Gorton, the "nice" American in *The Sun Also Rises* who accompanies Jake Barnes on a significantly therapeutic fishing trip, a pastoral oasis if there ever was one. The equivalent now of pastoral shepherds are the Basque peasants, denominated "a swell people" by Bill. One of them, a woman selling liquor, is so simple and innocent she's never heard of tipping. Jake having given her ten centimes extra, "she gave me back the copper piece," he says, "thinking I had misunderstood the price." But Bill and Jake enter the real oasis further on, as they step into a shady wood. Shade trees are an all but indispensable fixture of genuine literary pastoral. Ruhe illustrates from Theocritus, Virgil, and finally Spenser, who recalls the end of Virgil's *First Eclogue* in "December":

The gentle shepheard sat beside a springe,
All in the shadowe of a bushy brere. . . .

And Ruhe adds: "The engraver of the early Spenser woodcuts took pains to supply most of the illustrations with shade trees, as well as emblems of wilderness and of habitations, as if to affirm again and again the middle zone [between barbarism, on the one hand, and urbanity on the other] which pastoral shepherds occupy."

Jake Barnes describes a wood the two pass through on their way to the fishing stream:

> It was a beech wood and the trees were very old. Their roots bulked above the ground and the branches were twisted. We walked on the road between the thick trunks of the old beeches and the sunlight came through the leaves in light patches on the grass. The trees were big, and the foliage was thick but it was not gloomy. There was no undergrowth, only the smooth grass, very green and fresh, and the big gray trees well spaced as though it were a park.

(Impossible not to recall the Forest of Arden.) Hemingway's shade trees happen to be beeches, and we may remember the similar imagery in Thomas Gray's *Elegy;* the visitor to the churchyard is told of the rural epitaph-writer,

There at the foot of yonder nodding beech
That wreathes its old fantastic roots so high,

His listless length at noontide would he stretch,
And pore upon the brook that babbles by.

Beech trees too are the species invoked by Siegfried Sassoon in a neopastoral poem occasioned by the death of his friend David Thomas in the First World War. The poem, "A Letter Home," was written in 1916 and addressed to Robert Graves, who also knew David Thomas. Sassoon cannot bear the thought of David dead. His consolation is to fancy him resurrected in the spring and available to the imagination as a sort of male dryad. He tells Graves,

We've been sad because we've missed
One whose yellow head was kissed
By the gods, who thought about him
Till they couldn't do without him.
Now he's here again; I've seen
Soldier David dressed in green,
Standing in a wood that swings
To the madrigal he sings. . . .
Yes, it's certain, here he teaches
Outpost-schemes to groups of beeches.

And one of the latest appearances of beech trees as pastoral props is in Philip Roth's brilliant novel of 1986, *The Counterlife*, where his fantasied wife, Maria, with whom he quarrels over her preference for "pastoral," as opposed to his for "contradiction or conflict," reveals some beloved places of her innocent girlhood: "One was a beech woods where she used to go for walks."

The scene of which Hemingway's beeches are a part draws from Bill the uncomplex ejaculation, "This is country." That is the reaction too of the principals in the film *The Deer Hunter* to the high, clean mountain country they recreate themselves in just before plunging into the violence of the Vietnam War. Bill and Jake are taking pastoral refuge as well, from the violence and incoherence and mess of expatriate life in Paris and Pamplona. "We can hardly have extended pastoral fictions," Ruhe observes, "without [implied contrasting] violence and other strongly counter-pastoral elements." "I was through with fiestas for a while," says Jake after the madness and noise and excitement of Pamplona. Recoiling, he travels alone to the Spanish beach oasis—resort town, actually—of San Sebastian. There he purges and simplifies, swimming out in the cold water to a raft where two pastoral lovers enter the framed picture: "A boy and girl were at the other end [of the raft]. The girl had undone the top strap of her bathing-suit and was browning her back. The boy lay face downward on the raft and talked to her. She laughed at things he said, and turned her brown back in the sun." (In observing that the picture is as if framed, I have recalled the customary etymological interpretation of Theocritus's title *Idylls* as "little pictures.") Their innocence is a distinct relief after the frenzied erotics of Pamplona, associated notably with the nymphomaniacal aristocrat Lady Brett Ashley. Located socially at the furthest distance urban sophistication can place her from these two innocent pastoral lovers on the raft at San Sebastian, she stands as a doubtless unwitting example of the aristocrat for whom, as William Empson argues, pastoral literature was contrived in the first place.

"The locus of pastoral is at the margin of civilization," notes Ruhe. The beach, no matter how comfortably furnished, may be thought a convenient emblem of such a margin, as Jake Barnes's suntanning boy and girl suggest. Because in its earlier form pastoral, as the obverse of epic, registers the desire to enjoy a holiday from the strains of ambition and the pressure of destructively competing social groups, in its displaced form the pastoral urge will invite us to a holiday at the beach. It is curious that as a venue of pleasure and relaxation, a place from which you return "refreshed," the beach began to be popular only when the demise of formal literary pastoral had taken place.

But for the beach to become desirable as a new "pastoral" setting, the sun had to be rehabilitated as a wholly beneficial force. In the days of Matthew Arnold's *Thyrsis* and *The Scholar Gypsy,* the sun had borne a sad social stigma. Aristocrats especially had shunned it, women and girls of the upper orders carefully protecting their faces from it with parasols and wide-brimmed hats and their hands with gloves. But at the very outset of the twentieth century things began to change. As early as 1902 André Gide, in *L'Immoraliste,* depicted the tubercular Michel deriving magic benefit from sunbathing, and later one of Gide's faithful readers, Hermann Hesse, imitated Michel, sunbathing in Italy as a specific against his headaches and gout. The late-Victorian German nudist movement began as a form of therapy but soon turned recreational, and stripping down to minimal clothing became an indispensable part of what Ruhe has called "the pleasance paradigm." At the beach, "disburdening" notably takes place, a remote but recognizable analogue to the disburdening (of civic sophistication, etc.) by which the characters in literary pastoral signal their happy remoteness from a corrupt urbanism.

The whole movement by which the rays of the sun were found beneficial after centuries of rejection has been called, by John Weightman, the Solar Revolution, and it constitutes one of the most startling reversals in modern intellectual and emotional history. In the nineteenth century the "poetic" heavenly body was, by common consent, the moon—and it was so recognized by poets like Tennyson and Poe. But by the early twentieth century it was conventionally the sun that projected mystical emanations, and "to be a child of the sun," as the idiom of the period put it, was the impulse governing scores of intellectuals, writers, and artists, including Ezra Pound's Hugh Selwyn Mauberley, who fantasizes an escape from urbanism and commercial corruption, bringing him to a place of "Thick foliage/Placid beneath warm suns." For the Stephen Spender who went to Germany after the First World War partly to enjoy the sunbathing craze there, "the life of the senses was a sunlit garden from which," like pastoral, "sin was excluded."

For Europeans and Americans, the Mediterranean coast rapidly became the favored place for disburdening, and the style of its beach resorts was soon providing the model for the décor of successful international tourism. Wherever exported and transplanted out of Europe—to Turkey, Mexico, even the Soviet Union—the style is the same, involving beach and sun, copious food and humble wine easily come by, and folk music (played less often now on pipes than on string instruments). There will often be inhabitants living closer to the pastoral ideal even than the tourists—colorful fishermen and boat people, devotees of harmless pastimes like *boules* or something similar. After lunch, there must be innocent love on top of the sheets and innocent sleep preparing the pastoralists for further programmed disburdening. The scene, constituting one of the main presiding myths of the desirable for the modern urban imagination, is identifiable as the postindustrial world's version of pastoral, its "pleasance paradigm." It is recognizable as a displacement of the former image of the longed-for, the traditional pastoral scene of quiet inland waters, shade trees, sheep-filled meadows, and silence broken only by the songs of shepherds or birds. As if recognizing the degree to which the conventional modern vacation site has dis- (or re-) placed the former image of the desirable in nature registered by literary pastoral, one cartoonist for *The New Yorker* has recently depicted a middle-class couple planning a holiday. While the wife studies vacation brochures, the husband, as if remembering numerous failed bucolic holidays in the past, barks out: "And for God's sake, no more meadows full of sheep." The duties of shepherds, Ruhe reminds us, "are the lightest possible in the world of human work," and the contemporary observer of rows of sunbathers at a beach resort will note a similarity. Fontenelle, says Ruhe, "assessed the life of Arcadian shepherds as ideally lazy; and indeed it borders on idleness and irresponsibility little short of inertness and stupor." Ruhe's term for the former pastoral world is "the rural-euphoric": we might term this later version of it the Littoral Euphoric.

202 — PAUL FUSSELL

And the way pastoral characters tend less to act than to be acted upon, whether trailing their sheep from hill to hill or, as sunbathers, supine and actionless, receiving the sun's rays, seems underlined by the very passive voice of Philip Roth's (or Nathan Zuckerman's) reprehension of the pastoral, which, he says, begins in "those irrepressible yearnings by people . . . *to be taken off* to the perfectly safe, charmingly simple and satisfying environment that is desire's homeland."

"The antidote for civilization": that could be thought a not too inaccurate designation of literary pastoralism. But actually it is the current advertising slogan of Club Méditerranée, which is in the business of enticing the over-urbanized to a world resembling the pastoral in certain remarkable respects: "Today at Club Med," says its advertising brochure, "there are no time schedules to live by because there are no clocks. No budgets to adhere to because there is no money." Like pastoral, "For every pressure of civilization, Club Med has a release." It is a perfect contemporary incarnation of pastoral's perpetual Other. And it is no accident that the bulk of Club Méditerranée's resorts are located on beaches. Not likely to go on that kind of vacation but still not immune to the quasi-pastoral appeal of beach imagery are the impoverished Joe Buck and Rico Rizzo of the film *Midnight Cowboy,* which unremittingly opposes "Miami Beach" to "New York City," offering the image of the distant beach as the ultimate totem of felicitous escape.

During the 1960s, while writing books on Thomas Hardy and Henry James, Irving Howe fled every summer to Cape Cod, which, he testifies, "became my pastoral." His statement may suggest the degree to which pastoral imagining lies behind his and other intellectuals' socialistic utopianism, and may point to the survival of pastorality in much Western agitation for political and social reform. A remarkable number of mid-twentieth-century anthropological studies resemble displaced pastorals in their Rousseauist, sentimental-primitivist attitude toward aborigines. And the same can be said of many recent works of humanistic intellect or scholarship, like Robert Coles's *William Carlos Williams: The Knack of Survival in America,* where the pastoral model for personality and character—that is, simplicity and instinctive virtue—tends to dominate Coles's interpretations of literary characters and motives.

Traditional pastoral writing tends to define virtue as the absence of acquisitiveness. Shepherds are not traders, they have no visible money, nor are dowries a part of marriage understandings. In the modern capitalistic world, retirement from a life of trade usually betokens a new degree of relative poverty and simplicity. The current rhetoric of retirement suggests the displacement of pastoral themes there. *Travel and Retirement Edens Abroad*—thus the title of a best-seller of 1983. The term *community* in the phrase Retirement Community suggests much of the appeal extended by the image of the benign noncompetitive; and outlining some of the features of the pastoral *locus amoenus,* Ruhe again sheds light on another persistent pastoral image, that of final happiness to be found in a "retirement community." "The shepherd pleasance," he notes, "has the safety of a nest, the euphoria of a dream, and the comfort of a reliable, reassuring, frictionless community."

"The woods of Arcady are dead," complained William Butler Yeats's "Last Arcadian" in 1889:

> The woods of Arcady are dead,
> And over is their antique joy;
> Of old the world on dreaming fed;
> Grey truth is now her painted toy.

But to look closely at a number of contemporary phenomena is to know better. The world never ceases to feed on dreams, and truth has never been her toy. The world is a thing that always requires compensatory imagery to make it acceptable, and "pastoral" is as good a word as any to suggest the form compensatory imagery is likely, universally, to assume. "Human kind/Cannot bear very much reality," says Eliot, echoing the findings of Freud in *Civilization and Its Discontents*. Poggioli is speaking of pastoral poetry, but he could just as well be describing all the acts of imagination and impulse through which we can perceive the persistence of pastoral when he writes, "[Pastoral] . . . performs with especial intensity the role that Freud assigns to art in general: that of acting as a vicarious compensation for the renunciations imposed by the social order on its individual members, and of reconciling men to the sacrifices they have made in civilization's behalf."

TAKING IT
ALL OFF
IN THE
BALKANS

If enjoying the beach is the most common contemporary enactment of the pastoral urge, enjoying the beach nude is the ultimate form. What could more conveniently constitute an antidote to civilization and a celebration of Golden Age honesty, freedom, and simplicity than casting off your dearest disguises? And casting off as well that sly, niggling, self-conscious, crypto-porno sexualism which is as telling a stigma of Modernism as free verse or anthropology? You don't believe you slough off sexual obsession when you take off your clothes in public? Come with me to the Balkans.

"Yugoslavia," a state tourist official said recently, "is becoming one great nude beach." But it hasn't reached that goal yet—there are still other attractions: Sarajevo, with its minarets and the bridge where a few pistol shots started the First World War; the town of Cetinje, capital of the former midget country of Montenegro, its once pretentious British and Russian and Turkish embassies fallen into ironic ruin. And of course Belgrade, Split, Zagreb, and the superb walled city of Dubrovnik. Once it was named Ragusa, and its merchant marine was the rival of Venice. The word *argosy* comes from its former name. But finally you're bound to wander up and down the coast, and it's there you can sense what the tourist-industry spokesman is getting at. It's a good place to experience, if you haven't already, the manners and unwritten rules governing communal naturism. Or nudism, as it used to be called when there seemed something naughty and furtive about it. Once, no more than twenty-five years ago, people who went to "nudist camps" were careful to use only their first names. Now, no such caution.

If you're curious, the best place in the whole world to take the pulse of international naturism is the Adriatic Coast —totaling 3,700 miles, islands and inlets included—of the Socialist Federal Republic of Yugoslavia. It has been in the nude-beach business (*nudizma,* in Serbo-Croat) for over twenty-five years, less to set a good example of personal liberty to other Communist countries than to earn lots of foreign exchange. Chiefly Deutsche Marks. For the past few years West Germany has supplied the bulk of visitors to

Yugoslavia, followed by Britain, France, Czechoslovakia, Belgium, Holland, and Italy. Afflicted with sexual anxieties as they are known to be, nice Republican middle-class Americans—those, that is, with the money and the motive to travel around Europe—have not responded wildly to the naturist invitation. You almost never see Yanks in take-it-all-off Yugoslavian settings, although in their baggy shorts and frilly one-pieces they can sometimes be observed glancing wistfully toward areas designated FOR NUDISTS ONLY: ALL OTHERS KEEP AWAY.

Actually the naturist beaches are so German that they seem all but exclusively so, and the local socialist barkeeps and waitresses and windsurfing instructors have learned long ago that *Bier* means *pivo; Weisswein, belo vino;* and *bitte, molim.* The vast throngs of German naturists are assisted by their own guidebooks to Dalmatian *Naktkultur,* like *Naktfakte,* a work listing the best naturist beaches, hotels, camp sites, and resorts. Driving, the German tourist has only to follow the signs reading FKK to find the right beaches. FKK, a term which may sound a bit suggestive to English speakers, is simply an abbreviation of *Freikörperkultur,* a word invented around the 1920s by the Germans to invest the whole nudist operation with an air of the therapeutic and the innocent-educational. The FKK sign will lead the traveler to some thirty naturist sites along the coast, ranging from simple unimproved tent sites and trailer camps to elaborate hotels and even small towns. From a distance, these towns appear quite ordinary, but when you come closer you see everyone going around stark naked, shopping at the supermarket and the drugstore, sipping apéritifs at the café, going to the hairdressers, renting sailboats for the day, or driving off in the family car for a picnic.

For a typical naturist experience you might go to the Hotel Osmine, near the small town of Slano, twenty-five miles north of Dubrovnik. This is a standard, moderate-priced family resort hotel of some three hundred rooms, with the usual dining room, bar, and game room. As you register you may notice that virtually every passport in the cubby-holes is West German. The nice elderly woman at the desk reminds you—a bit gingerly, since you are American and thus, doubtless, in her view a puritan and moral dogmatist, quite ready to be shocked—that this is a naturist hotel. Any doubt on this score will vanish as you walk down a long stairway and approach the beach, where all normal activity —swimming and sailing lessons, beer drinking, or lunching at the café—is taking place without bathing suits and with no self-consciousness or visible sexual awareness whatever. Ages ranges from one to eighty-five years, and everyone is brown. All over.

Is only the beach naturist, or is the whole hotel? Offi-cially, the whole hotel is, but you notice that as people return from the beach, they gradually begin covering up, and only a rare naturist (an impudent one, some would say) arrives back at the public rooms with nothing on. I did see two middle-aged men nude at the bar, but it didn't look right, and even they seem embarrassed. When the sun disappears, so does naturism. In the dining room at evening and for dancing on the patio at night, everyone is dressed, just as if the place were a normal hotel. But in the morning, off it all comes again as you head for the sand and the water. The boys in the dance band, nicely dressed for their performance the night before, are seen on the beach the next day, politely greeting everyone. They are now nude.

What does it feel like, taking it all off in public? At first, to be sure, there's a terrible shyness, and you spend a lot of effort worrying about the most decent way to disrobe. (This is before you come to understand that the term *decent* belongs to an anxious world which is not this one.) Should your shorts or your shirt be the last thing you remove? Experience will inform you that removing shorts or bathing suit *first* is the more honorable way. Once stripped, you sense a momentary impulse to Look Your Best—stand straight, shoulders back. Pull in that stomach. But after a few minutes of this, you understand that you've missed the whole point, and you relax as the genuine naturist feeling begins to flood over you. The naturist feeling? A new and lovely sense of perfect freedom, not just from jocks and waistbands and bras but from social fears and niggling gentilities. You quickly overcome your standard anxieties about what the neighbors or the boss will think. The illusion, which naturists recognize as an illusion, is that all evil has been for the moment banished from the beach. Including the grave risk of skin cancer, which is never mentioned by naturists.

On naturist premises you notice all sorts of significant things about people. You notice first something easily obscured in artificial or sophisticated circles, namely, that everyone is unequivocally male or female, and that effeminate or butch mannerisms don't do much to define identity and character once the drapes are put aside. You become aware too that the "unisex" concept is a fraud and a delusion, a con useful to merchandising and perhaps to sentimentality but useful nowhere else. To the naturist eye, men are men and women are women, and there's no way to shade or qualify the difference.

Nude, older people look younger, especially when very tan, and younger people look even younger—almost like infants, some of them. In addition fat people look far less offensive naked than clothed. Clothes, you realize, have the effect of sausage casings, severely defining and advertising the shape of what they contain, pulling it all into an unnatural form which couldn't fool anyone. And there's one visual side benefit of naturism that those with taste will appreciate: the eye is repulsed much less than in normal vacation life by those hideous "resort" clothes. No one is got up in bright green pseudo-linen Bermuda shorts or self-humiliating hundred-dollar knit shirts celebrating the male tits of the too-well-fed middle-aged, or horrible "Italian" brown and white shoes with holes and cutouts. Better total nakedness: no one totally nude could look as ugly as someone costumed in current vacation wear, no matter his or her shape. The beginning naturist doesn't take long to master the principle that it is stockings that make varicose veins noticeable, belts that call attention to forty-eight-inch waists, brassieres that emphasize sagging breasts. Not to mention the paradox, familiar to all naturists, that the body clothed is really sexier than the body nude. As one experienced naturist notes, "Much of our clothing . . . tends to accentuate certain areas of the body that it is supposed to hide." That's part of the pleasure of clothes, of course, but there's pleasure also in rejecting that convention in favor of one that proves in practice to involve an unaccustomed sort of innocence.

A further benefit of naturism is this: you regain something of the physical unselfconsciousness and absence of anxiety about your appearance that you had as a young child. A little time spent on naturist beaches will persuade most women that their breasts and hips are not, as they may think when alone, appalled by their mirrors, "abnormal," but quite natural, "abnormal" ones belonging entirely to the nonexistent creatures depicted in ideal painting and sculpture. The same with men: if you think nature has been unfair to you in the sexual anatomy sweepstakes, spend some time among the naturists. You will learn that every man looks roughly the same—quite small, that is, and that heroic fixtures are not just extremely rare, they are deformities.

In their enthusiasm to forward a noble cause in a suspicious, nasty-minded world, naturists have been vigorous devisers of euphemisms. *Naturist* has by now virtually ousted *nudist,* which itself could be supposed a sort of euphemism for *nakedist.* Lest the idea of a *naturist beach* seem too jolting to the conventional, naturists have come up with *free beach,* or *clothing-or-swimsuit-optional beach. Sunbathing* is popular as a disarming synonym for *nudism,* and among the cognoscenti no elbow nudge is needed to suggest how it differs from *sunning,* which is what you do with a bathing suit on. Indeed, the diction of nudism could supply material for a good-sized study. In Australia, it is *sunbaking* that means taking the sun nude. *Sunbathing* there means with a bathing suit on. Beaches where cover-up is required are now often referred to, by naturists, as *textile* beaches, as opposed to both *top-free* and simply *free*. Europeans are more likely to use terms involving some form of the word nude. In America, nudist clubs and resorts are united by membership in the American Sunbathing Association or the Naturist Society. But regardless of what you call it, ideas not just of sun but of water seem indispensable to the movement. Even confirmed naturists might feel uncomfortable stripping indoors or in some conventionally unwholesome and unathletic environment like a cocktail lounge, say, or a poolroom.

People don't just (forgive the understatement) look different on a naturist beach. They act different. And actually the code of manners governing naturist behavior is about the most formal to be met with in the current social scene. People accustomed to backslapping, touching, or asking all and sundry "Where you from?" or "Come here often?" will be startled to find the atmosphere of a nude beach as decorous as that of the Back Bay about 1910.

The rules are nowhere available for study, but they are apparent to all, and if you don't catch on fast, the naturists will urge you to leave. For one thing, no staring. Or, more accurately, no conspicuous staring. Permitted is genteel staring from behind dark glasses or when looking up occasionally from reading. A more specific visual no-no: when conversing, you look nowhere but at the face of the person addressed. But it's best to address no one but your partner, if any, and you should never go wandering about, in quest of "dates." Cameras are not very popular, and a habitual naturist will recoil from the sight of one the way a good Moslem flinches from a bottle of vodka. But if cameras are frowned upon, so equally is any show of "modesty," which has meaning, after all, only in the world of dress. For the naturist the ideal presentation is the air of everything being quite normal. You should act as if you always go around with no clothes on. You should give the impression that you would be scandalized to hear that the practice strikes some people as odd or perverse. But there is one crucial, and interesting, exception to the antimodesty convention.

Some philosphes of the eighteenth century, anxious to demonstrate that Whatever Is, Is Right, argued that in planning the human body Nature must have known exactly what she was doing, for she took care to hide from customary view the least prepossessing external body opening. Naturists seem to recognize at least the aesthetic element of this argument, for they seem careful never to let the audience to the rear see them bending down. In fact, that undignified, even comical, part of the body is never knowingly exposed by a naturist, a fact suggesting that even naturism retains its pruderies, for all its pretense of bravely casting them aside.

Contrary to the ordinary frequenter of "textile" beaches, naturists consider their turfs not at all appropriate theaters of eroticism. "Naturism and pornography," one naturist pointed out recently, "are irreconcilable." A spokesman for Polish naturism has asserted: "With our beach nudity we protest against the perversion of erotic life, that is, against pornography and refined exhibitionism." In the United States there is now an organization called NOPE (Naturists Opposing Pornographic Exploitation) devoted to publicizing the nonerotic element in social naturism. Naturists cannot be compared to exhibitionists either, because of the vigorous contempt they feel for peepers, whether by land, peering down from cliffs through binoculars, or by sea, cutting in too close to the beach in small boats, and giggling lewdly. Naturists regard all such people as sick and in need of treatment. They also deeply resent the presence on their beaches of the clothed, be the clothing ever so slight (except, of course, for the hotel or beach staff, whose clothing makes them easy to spot when you need their services). It's amazing the way a bikini, even if both top and bottom are present, looks grossly obscene in a nude context, nastily coy and flirtatious. To a naturist, the toplessness of French beaches is the ultimate pornography. Jewelry, on the other hand, is permitted so long as, like earrings and crosses on gold chains, it is not trying to conceal anything normally considered sexually meaningful. By the same token hats are allowed, and, on rocky beaches, shoes.

The naturist attitude toward more extensive covering up will suggest the essential nudist emotion and value: "sincerity." It is this that prompts women to leave off makeup: too suggestive of fraud and archness. And in addition to sincerity, and perhaps harder to believe, innocence. A sixteenth-century painting by Lucas Cranach can illustrate that point. It is titled *The Golden Age,* that is, before the fall of humankind into dirtymindedness, and the version in the Alte Pinakothek, Munich, depicts eleven couples disporting nude in a scene that could almost be a naturist beach. They are swimming, chatting, and dancing hand-in-hand around a tree, and the naturalness and innocence of their nudity is underlined by the presence of a "naturist" lion couple and

Lucas Cranach the Elder, *The Golden Age* (Alte Pinokothek, Munich)

deer couple, both clearly devoid of foul-minded sexual innuendo.

As opposed to its shy beginnings a half century or more ago, naturism currently has acquired strength and purpose and a degree of high privilege from ecological, environmentalist, and conservationist movements, of which naturists easily feel themselves a significant part. All these impulses, after all, constitute votes on behalf of "the natural," to be preserved and valued as a quasi-religious obligation. Littering, thus, is quite unthinkable to naturists, as irreconcilable with social nudity as pornography. As one longtime practitioner says, naturism occupies a central position between purposeless nudism and love-of-outdoor-things naturalism. A naturist, he points out, is not quite a naturalist, but almost. One Italian naturist, describing a nudist lake shore not far from Rome, says, "Here, people seek naturism. They don't disturb or pollute. The lake keeps its integrity."

Sooner or later, anyone reading about this topic is bound to wonder about what one may call the Male Response. The fact is that if one pursues one's naturism correctly, it's no problem at all. Dealing with it, making sure it doesn't happen, is precisely a part of the naturist exercise, indeed, one of its benefits, if one may go so far as that. The naturist rule, No Love in Public, helps keep one on the right track. Naturists agree that, given the cascades of sexual stimuli poured over us by contemporary civilization, at stated times and places a little contrived, conscious sexlessness is good for you.

For all its essential charm and harmlessness, not everyone is enthusiastic about naturism in Yugoslavia. The prim British travel writer J. A. Cuddon has produced a *Companion Guide to Jugoslavia* whose 480 pages do not once mention that naturism is an attraction, although he includes sections on Principal Coastal Resorts, Hotels, Entertainment, Spas, and

Costumes, and devotes 162 pages to a description of the Dalmatian Coast. (It may be worth noting that when it comes to priggish, self-righteous, "middle-class" disapproval of naturism, it is likely that British lips are doing the uttering. Like Valerie Grove's, who recently deplored, in the *Spectator,* the growing popularity of naturism in the Mediterranean. Argument failing her, she descends to physical insult, assuming that the main naturist motive is simple exhibitionism:

> As for the full frontal men lying stretched out, what poor bare fork'd things indeed. It was my mother-in-law who declared that the problem here is one of visibility. Perhaps some sort of magnifying glass could be provided, she suggests?

It's pleasant to observe that such smirking, self-satisfied puritanism becomes rarer each year, although it doubtless disappears more slowly from the former Anglo-Saxon empires than elsewhere. Valerie Grove's reaction nicely illustrates Orwell's point about geographical righteousness, which applies as well to Canadians, Americans, and Mexicans, in that order. "When nationalism first became a religion, the English looked at the map, and, noticing that their island lay very high in the Northern Hemisphere, evolved the pleasing theory that the further north you live the more virtuous you are.")

From J. A. Cuddon and his like you'd never gather that several travel agencies, like Yugotours (see any big-city Yellow Pages), offer complete naturist package tours to Yugoslavia. For example, Lister International Travel advertises a seventeen-day tour attractively named The Adriatic Escapade. This conveys people "with an insatiable sense of curiosity to try new things" to a number of the naturist coastal resorts, "the ideal place to acquire the ultimate suntan."

The naturist coast is largely a Roman Catholic area. I wondered about the attitude of the faithful and others who might be thought to disapprove of all this, and I sought some illumination from the Director of Tourism for the Dubrovnik area. He assured me that the Church gave no trouble, and couldn't even if it wanted to, because, thanks to socialism—i.e., communism—the Church was no longer a power in Yugoslavia. He pointed out that even in Greece, where at least in rural areas the Orthodox Church is still potent, the Church has been unable to reverse the modern trend to touristic naturism. Why expect the Church to have greater power in a socialist country? Yes, but how does naturism square with socialism? (I was thinking of the quasi-capitalistic cynical profit-making behind the whole operation.) It squares perfectly, he said, rather heatedly: socialism is founded upon mutual respect among human beings, and if you want to take your clothes off, who am I to object, so long as you don't force me to look at the spectacle?

He pointed out also that socialism concerns itself with the public health and that naturism has been held to have distinct therapeutic value. Indeed, he went on, some Yugoslavian physicians prescribe swimming at naturist resorts as a cure for barrenness in women. It is the therapeutic benefits of naturism that are specified in the official 24-page pamphlet *Jugoslavia Naturism,* issued by the National Tourist Office. Yugoslavia, it says, was among the first countries to encourage naturists to pursue "their useful cause which contributes to a person's spiritual and physical well-being." So important is Yugoslavia in the whole naturist movement that in 1972 the World Naturist Congress chose to hold its convention there, the equivalent, we are to assume, of the American Medical Association deciding to meet in Boston or Rochester, Minnesota, or the Medieval Academy of America deciding to meet in Canterbury. Whatever the reason, there's something about European communism in general that seems interestingly hospitable to naturism. The reason is probably in part communism's readiness to do things that annoy religious institutions and other survivals of "feudal" values. Hungary, for example, seems rapidly catching up to Yugoslavia as a naturist paradise, and a large gathering of international naturists chose to honor it by assembling there in 1987. Even Poland, despite the troubles communism encounters there from the Church and the citizenry, goes in for a surprising amount of naturism, the total number of devotees there being estimated as between 100,000 and 200,000.

I left the Director of Tourism quite buoyed up about the future of naturism. Since Yugoslavia already has some naturist towns, would there ultimately be naturist cities? And how about naturist countries? There dirty shows might consist of women on sleazy platforms slowly and slyly putting on clothes.

"Yugoslavia's 1,000-island Dalmatian Coast is the most beautiful in the world." So says the Lister Tours naturist holiday brochure, and for once a travel agency is not lying, or even exaggerating. Naturism is a success along the Balkan Adriatic because there nature is a success. The coastline is incredibly lovely—low hills, pine trees and palms, unpolluted water, benign dark blue sea, brilliant skies, caressing sun. There the squalid, which might threaten naturism, seems drained away, leaving only innocent beauty. You get the feeling that if naturism is grand and even (permit me) ennobling near Slano, it would be degrading near Camden or Detroit.

Sea and sky and sun, and after swimming and browning all day, all over, in the evening cold lobster with mayonnaise and the local light white wine. And never any wet bathing suits to hang up. Not a bad formula for something like heaven, an attainable version of superpastoral.

THE FATE
OF CHIVALRY
AND THE
ASSAULT
UPON MOTHER

I have already adverted to the Solar Revolution, that startling turnaround in the public attitude toward the sun and its effects on human beings which is one signal of the modern era. Another is what can be called the chivalric revolution, although perhaps *revulsion* would be a better word.

The idea of chivalry I'm thinking of derives from the romanticizing of the Middle Ages that occurred in the later eighteenth century, a phenomenon marked by the Gothic Revival in architecture and decoration, the vogue of "Ossian" and Gothic fiction, and the recovery of Chaucer. A century later an even more intense form of this sentimental archaism was promoted by Victorian aesthetes. Saturated in Arthurian themes and deeply conservative and patriotic, they were reacting against utilitarianism, industrialism, agnosticism, and socialism. The Victorian celebration of the chivalric is an attempt by the traditional imagination to posit that the modern world, with its political compromises and gross materialism, its scientism and urban squalor and proletarianization, does not exist.

This Victorian form of the chivalric understanding comprises a rich amalgam of archaic images and behavioral imperatives. These are drawn from such materials as *The Song of Roland,* Malory's *Morte d'Arthur, Sir Gawain and the Green Knight,* Chaucer's *Knight's Tale,* Michael Drayton's *The Battle of Agincourt,* Spenser's *Faerie Queene,* and Shakespeare's *Henry V,* as well as from works by such latter-day popularizers of medieval materials as Tennyson and William Morris. First, there is a hankering after knightly trappings, and here Robinson's Miniver Cheevy is a good example of the chivalric archaizer. He

> loved the days of old
>   When swords were bright and steeds were prancing;
> The vision of a warrior bold
>   Would set him dancing.

The chivalric imagination exults in armor, stained glass, cottage manufacture, baldrics, castles, moats, drawbridges, portcullises, drums, trumpets, and bugles, and it likes to conceive torches being passed from the hands of "the fallen" to those who continue the struggle. Since the chivalric practitioner of the olden time was most often mounted, horses and their accouterments are indispensable. Nobility is imputed to them as well as their riders, requiring them to be referred to as *steeds* or *chargers*. (It would have to be on a *charger* that Sir Walter Scott's Young Lochinvar spirits his love away.) And in bellicose contexts horses are attended with all the romantic habiliments of cavalry, like lances, pennons, guidons, and sabers.

A crucial chivalric imperative is fairness, even disinterestedness, in combat: the enemy must be given an equal chance and treated fairly and honorably. Which is to say that the chivalrous man, like Wordsworth's Happy Warrior, "keeps the law." An equally important element of the chivalric code is the ennobling of women, as in Tennyson. Their honor is precious, and some of them are so noble that they are virtually saints already. Wounded and in the hospital, one Canadian officer of the Great War, author of the book *The Glory of the Trenches,* testifies that the nurses were "Arthurian": "I see them as great ladies," he writes, "medieval in their saintliness, sharing the pollution of the battle with their champions." Very like the Boy Scout, whose twelve-point code apes the knightly one (as imagined by Victorian reactionaries), a knight is reverent, and if he resembles Galahad, he can achieve actual holiness. Since when on a crusade the knight opposes the enemies of Christianity, his death in battle is an act of Christ-like sacrifice, wholly noble and redemptive. In his famous sonnet "The Dead," Rupert Brooke specifies "holiness," in addition to "honor" and "nobleness," as gifts the dead British soldiers convey to the yet living ones. Indeed, the dead have managed to reverse the course of progress and cultural modernism, and

> . . . we have come into our heritage,

that is, retrograde, chivalric conceptions of soldiering.

Again, the knight is loyal and obedient to his superiors. He reveres his monarch, honors the conventions of the *comitatus,* and is ready at all times to sacrifice himself for his military and social betters (usually identical). The Victorian and Edwardian kind of chivalry throve, of course, on the mystique of monarchy, and in 1914 virtually every European country—France and Switzerland excepted—could display an actual monarch. Indeed, at the outbreak of the Great War, it was still a "lingering notion," as Maurice Rickards has observed, that the monarch should be present on the battlefield. In admittedly backward Russia, the Czar actually was from time to time, which, some cynic might suggest, helps explain why the Russians did so badly. (In the same way, the same cynic might imply, the disaster of Dunkirk seems not unrelated to the late presence in France of the former almost-crowned head the Duke of Windsor, who, in British army uniform, dispensed advice and counsel.) The atmosphere of social hierarchy indispensable to the traditional imagination makes it seem natural for Gerard Manley Hopkins, in "The Windhover," to apostrophize a creature who is at once a kestrel and Christ as "O my chevalier!" Browning and Tennyson provide abundant examples of exemplary chivalric obedience. In Browning's "Incident of the French Camp" the badly wounded boy messenger—mounted, of course— brings to Napoleon the news of a crucial local victory and then, "smiling" proudly, falls dead. And in the Tennysonian model, "The Charge of the Light Brigade," the six hundred cavalrymen obey orders and ride to their death enthusiastically, even though they know that

Some one had blundered.

(Clearly someone high in the social hierarchy.)

A further tenet of the chivalric code requires sexual purity of the knight. The goal is *cleanliness*. Rupert Brooke's swimmers, welcoming the war in his sonnet "Peace," dive into cleanness, abjuring the "dirty songs and dreary" of "half-men." (Lytton Strachey?) In the same way, the soldiers in Robert Nichols's poem "The Day's March" achieve by means of military procedures a cleansing from "shame":

Heads forget heaviness,
Hearts forget spleen,
For by that mighty winnowing
Being is blown clean.
              • • •
And best! Love comes back again
After grief and shame. . . .

In a pamphlet titled *Cleansing London* (1915) the Bishop of London attacked the pimps swarming about the troops on leave and designated them "villains more mischievous than German spies, who ought to share their fate, [as they] lie in wait to stain the chivalry of our boys." There, *chivalry* functions as an elegant synonym for *chastity,* and that significance would be assumed by most contemporary admirers of George Frederic Watts's famous painting *Sir Galahad.* It's possible to sense that the storing up of semen is a prime source of physical, as well as moral, strength, when in Tennyson's "Sir Galahad," the noble youth testifies that his strength

> "Is as the strength of ten
> Because my heart is pure."

And if sexual purity is axiomatic in the chivalric code, so is total bravery. The idea of chivalry can admit of no neurasthenia, shell shock, combat fatigue, or post-traumatic stress disorder. And it can certainly admit of no running away, skulking, or scrimshanking.

This was the code of gentlemanly conduct with which the Anglo-Saxon allies were equipped in 1914. It is pleasantly available for study in Mark Girouard's *The Return to Camelot: Chivalry and the English Gentleman* (1981). At the outset there was no suspicion that very soon this code would appear ludicrously inappropriate, destined to defeat by poison gas, zeppelin raids on civilians, the machine gun, and unrestricted submarine warfare, not to mention such very unchivalric experiences as soldiers' passively trembling under artillery shelling hour after hour or soiling their trousers for weeks with acute dysentery (sometimes requiring the cutting of large holes in the rear of their clothing), or milking down their penises monthly before the eyes of bored and contemptuous medical officers alert for unreported gonorrheal discharges. Not to mention the unchivalric degradations intentionally visited upon modern conscripts in camps and billets. As Ivor Gurney complains in his poem "Servitude,"

To keep a brothel, sweep and wash the floor
Of filthiest hovels were noble to compare
With this brass-cleaning life. . . .

But when the war began no one suspected that chivalric imagery would encounter such rude modern realities.

In 1914 and 1915 allusion to the British at Agincourt was a ready way of suggesting a valuable chivalric continuity between the fifteenth-century battle, its sixteenth-century celebration by Drayton and Shakespeare, and the twentieth-century enactment of a presumably similar enterprise. It was the British archers of Agincourt whom Arthur Machen invoked in his famous fiction of the Angels of Mons, and a "fellowship" with the men of Agincourt is what is achieved by the once-timid clerk of Herbert Asquith's poem "The Volunteer." Before the war, this pathetic nonentity toiled at ledgers in the City, and his only access to high chivalric materials was through fantasy. But thanks to the war, he is able to encounter his "high hour" and, dead, he now goes to join the men of Agincourt,

gathered chivalrously into the British Valhalla. The dead British chivalry of the premodern world is invoked likewise in a patriotic poem of 1914 by Justin Huntly McCarthy, "Ghosts at Boulogne," which equates the British troops just landed in France with "Harry and His Crispins" and projects the British Expeditionary Force as a traditional heraldic and collective St. George, combating "the Worm"—the dragon of the Central Powers. The very titles of editorials in the London Times during September and October 1914, suggest the rhetorical atmosphere. On September 6 the lead editorial is titled "Courage." On September 20, "Chivalry." And on October 25, "Agincourt and the Modern Soldier."

It was the achievement of Robert Bridges, Poet Laureate, Platonist, and devotee of classical allusion, to impose the chivalric idea, normally associated with horses, onto the navy. In a poem titled "The Chivalry of the Sea" he designated the British navy as an institution fully equal in nobility to the cavalry, enforcing the point by indicating that sailors, after all, could be said to ride "iron coursers," from each of which the knightly sailors' "pennon flies." And Bridges's successor in the laureateship, John Masefield, went even further in the direction of chivalric associations. Because during the war he was a paid government propagandist, his wartime products suggest the degree to which the chivalric line was the official one. In writing his brief history Gallipoli, published in 1916, his obligation was to rationalize a disastrous campaign in which it might seem obvious that someone had blundered. An all but impossible task, one might think. But he was fortunate to find ready-made at Gallipoli a situation where the British, presumed Christians, were fighting the Turks, who were clearly "Paynims." He thus had before him an embroilment replicating the Crusades, and for Masefield a *crusade* constituted a useful metaphor, because one of his government's objects was to persuade the Americans to join a Christian war against barbarism. In order to suggest that the botched invasion of the Gallipoli Peninsula was really a contemporary crusade, Masefield invokes *The Song of Roland,* positioning a heroic quotation from that twelfth-century chivalric narrative as an epigraph at the head of each of his chapters. The actual Turks are thus made to blend with Roland's enemies, the Saracens, and the point can emerge that God is not on the Turks' side but on the Allies'. Actually, one could infer as much from their different standards of *purity.* "Our camps and trenches were kept clean," says Masefield. "But only a few yards away were the Turk trenches, which were invariably filthy; there the flies bred undisturbed, perhaps encouraged." Masefield pushes his Crusade analogy vigorously, at one point suggesting that the landing parties were virtually clad in white crusaders' tabards with red Christian crosses on the front. As the British troops approached the shore, death and wounds and hardship, says Masefield, "were but the end they asked, the reward they had come for, the unseen cross upon the breast." But finally even Masefield has to admit that the enterprise failed. That failure, however, is virtually irrelevant compared to the glory and heroism of the deeds it fortunately occasioned:

[The British troops] had failed to take Gallipoli, and the [Turkish] mine fields still barred the Hellespont, but they had fought a battle such as has never been seen upon this earth. What they had done will become a glory forever, wherever the deeds of heroic unhelped men are honored and pitied and understood.

And then Masefield delivers his final chivalric image: "They went up at the call of duty, with a bright banner of a battle-cry, against an impregnable fort." The skeptic, or even the military theorist, moved to ask, "Why on earth did they attack an impregnable position?" poses a question not to be presented to the chivalric imagination of 1916.

As Masefield's performance suggests, chivalric diction still carried a lot of weight with most people. Even though the war had been going on for two years and three months, to sentimentalists and Tories one still did not carry a rifle, one *bore arms.* The enemy was still *the host,* the battle *the tumult,* and actions *deeds,* rendered variously as *valiant, gallant,* or *noble.* Language like that had amazing staying power. Even in 1918 the Canadian Coningsby Dawson's title *The Glory of the Trenches* seems to have triggered very little rude laughter, although rude laughter at that sort of unwitting oxymoron is precisely what John Dos Passos's *Three Soldiers* (1921) invited. Actually, the medieval-minded Coningsby Dawson reviewed *Three Soldiers* in due course, and he was outraged, his outrage taking the form of chivalry insulted. Dos Passos's book, he wrote, constitutes "a dastardly denial of the splendid chivalry which carried many a youth to a soldier's death with the sure knowledge in his soul that he was a liberator."

The problem any writer faces who tries to reanimate the matter of chivalry to make it fit the actualities of the Great

War—or any other—becomes blindingly apparent in the face of the decline of military horse culture. Both linguistically and literally, the fate of chivalry implies the fate of cavalry. Words like *lancers* and *hussars* and *uhlans,* once conveying the clearest meaning and the warmest, most colorful associations, are now so obsolete as to require the coldest annotation. It was largely the machine gun, of course, that did for the cavalry as a plausible branch of the armed services. Once the static trench system was emplaced, cavalry units on both sides, deprived of their mission of assault and pursuit, disconsolately took their turns in the trenches as infantry, going back when rotated to care for their idle mounts well to the rear. They exercised their imaginations by envisaging the ultimate breakthrough, but after years of frustration they became as demoralized as anyone else and began to understand the fate of chivalry in the new world of industrialized warfare. One infantryman, a survivor of the attack on the Somme of July 1, 1916, asked for his strongest recollections of the day, perceived nothing but irony in the cavalry's readiness to perform their accustomed function: "My strongest recollection: all those grand looking cavalrymen, ready mounted to follow the breakthrough. What a hope!"

An acute intelligence spiced with a bit of skepticism might have inferred from nineteenth-century military history that as a weapon of mass attack cavalry had grown pitifully obsolete long before the Great War. There had been successful cavalry charges in the past, but to find one you'd have to go back as far as the Battle of Waterloo. But despite the data, the romance of chivalry persisted, and disasters like the charge of the Light Brigade, in 1854, became rather the rule than the exception. In 1866, in the Austro-Prussian War,

"56,000 cavalrymen," one authority points out, "armed only with sabers and lances, charged fatally into rifle- and gun-fire." The same thing happened in the Franco-Prussian War of 1870. But the romanticism of chivalry survived these pathetic demonstrations. The first commander-in-chief of the British forces in Belgium and France, Sir John French, had once provided a preface to the German General von Bern-hardi's book insisting on the indispensability of cavalry, and when the war broke out the Kaiser proclamed: "We shall resist to the last breath of man and horse." Throughout the war and despite the well-known actualities, the warhorse of chivalric tradition remained a standard feature of such ephemera as cigarette cards, postcards, and posters. The horse of battle was always noble and brave: he (she?) was thus an ethical model for the cavalryman. The horse was patient, too, as in Julian Grenfell's poem "Into Battle," written in 1915. Here "the fighting man" is befriended by all the forces of nature, especially the horse:

> In dreary, doubtful waiting hours,
>   Before the brazen frenzy starts,
> The horses show him nobler powers;
>   O patient eyes, courageous hearts!

But useless as the cavalry soon revealed itself to be, the chivalric associations of the very word lived on and on. It was found that some of the cavalry's dash could be salvaged and used to glorify aviators and their machines. Thus a book by Captain Alan Bott, MC, on the air forces: *Cavalry of the*

Clouds (1918). And as late as the 1940s the United States War Department announced, as if attempting to persuade the public that all was well and that the newest war was going to make safe, traditional sense, that the army had just supplied itself with 20,000 horses—the largest number, it emphasized, since the Civil War. That the cavalry idea dies as slowly as virtually any element of traditional imagining was further emphasized at the outset of the Second World War, when the Polish cavalry set out with impressive *élan* in September 1939, to repel the attack by panzers and Stukas. "As the Germans looked on in disbelief," says Robert Wernick,

> the troopers [of the crack Pomorske Cavalry Brigade] came riding . . . on splendid horses; white-gloved officers signalled the charge, trumpets sounded, pennons waved, sabers flashed in the sun. Like an animated page out of an old history book the brigade came forward across open fields, at a steady earth-shaking gallop, lances at the ready, straight into the fire of Guderian's tanks. In a few minutes the cavalry lay in a smoking, screaming mass of dismembered and disembowelled men and horses.

That was perhaps the last mass act in the history of chivalry, but with an idea so attractive, ministering so efficiently to the human desire that life be colorful and supremely interesting, one can never be sure that a timely death has overtaken it.

Discrediting it thoroughly was the object of the brilliant body of skeptical writing the Great War produced. These well-known satires and works of outrage seem to register the triumph of experience over theory, for the bitter poets, as well as the pissed-off novelists and memoirists, had all been up the line—as Rupert Brooke and John Masefield and Robert Bridges and the Bishop of London had not. The writings of Wilfred Owen, Robert Graves, Ernest Hemingway, and Siegfried Sassoon are all attacks on the chivalric model of warfare. Graves says good-bye to it in *Good-bye to All That,* Hemingway says farewell to it in *A Farewell to Arms.* Recuperating from wounds, Hemingway's Lieutenant Frederic Henry wanders into a military supply store in Milan. After be buys the pistol he needs, the woman owner asks, "Have you any need for a sword? I have some good used swords very cheap." "I'm going to the front," he answers, and she replies, in words sufficiently indicating the fate of chivalry, "Oh yes, then you won't need a sword."

In poetry, probably the best-known exposure of the irrelevance of chivalry is Owen's *"Dulce et Decorum Est,"* which comes fully alive as brutal monologue if one notices who the addressee is supposed to be. He—or just as likely she—is presumed to be ignorant, sentimental, bloodthirsty, and wholly loyal to the chivalric conception, and thus in severe need of noneuphemized instruction. If the reader could experience what the speaker has, if the chivalrous naïf could see what the speaker has seen, a gassed soldier dying disgustingly, with nothing of nobility attached to the act, the reader would no longer

> tell with such high zest
> To children ardent for some desperate glory,

The old lie: *Dulce et decorum est*
Pro patria mori.

The old lie was familiar, although of course not so designated
until Owen stigmatized it, to anyone who'd read Horace at
a Public School. Two decades before Owen wrote, it had
been highly popular as a patriotic goad during the Boer
War, and one of the poems recommending Horace's
tag, James Rhoades's *"Dulce et Decorum Est,"* may have
been Owen's specific target. Rhoades's *we* in these lines re-
fers to *we officers* who have been raised in traditions of chivalric honor:

We, nursed in high traditions,
And trained to nobler thought,
Deem death to be less bitter
Than life too dearly bought. . . .

And in May 1916, two months before the disastrous, instructive attack on the Somme, Sir Herbert Warren, president of
the Poetry Society (a source throughout the war of an uncomprehending chivalric view of events) offered in his Pres-
idential Address the suggestion that Tennyson's "The Charge
of the Light Brigade" was still a model for the sort of poetry
the war demanded, and he asserted as well that Horace's
dulce et decorum est pro patria mori (taken straight, of course)
should be the theme of all war poetry.

That position, and public rhetoric in general, has been
less damaged by Owen's utterance than the literate and the

skeptical might like to think. The American Purple Heart Medal still says "For Military Merit" on its obverse, although one earns it not for any action or decision but for having one's body accidentally penetrated by foreign objects. In 1918, the Somme area now cleared of the enemy, someone in authority in the Durham Light Infantry erected an elaborate twenty-foot-tall wooden memorial cross atop the notorious Butte of Warlencourt, a sinister terrain feature from which for years the Germans had dominated the battlefield. Words painted on the main part of the cross memorialize the men who "fell in the attack on the Butte of Warlencourt and Surrounding Trenches on Nov 5th and 6th, 1916." And then, in a circle around the intersection—it is a Celtic cross —the words *Dulce et decorum est pro patria mori.*" Did Owen ever see this cross? No, he wrote his poem a year before it was put up. Did those who set up the cross see his poem? No, it was not published until two years later. This is to suggest the unlikelihood, then and now, of the chivalric and the antichivalric taking much notice of each other. Despite the shock of the Somme and a thousand subsequent disillusions, the chivalric tradition, enfeebled and compromised though it may be, remains one of the attendants of social and political conservatism. For its part, the antichivalric impulse takes off in the opposite direction, its rude skepticisms helping to consolidate the gains of Modernism and Post-Modernism.

If Owen deflates Horace, Herbert Read deflates the Wordsworth who defined and celebrated the "Character of the Happy Warrior." Read's modern Happy Warrior is really the Unhappy Conscript, thoroughly victimized and unmanned by terror and hysteria:

THE HAPPY WARRIOR

His wild heart beats with painful sobs,
His strain'd hands clench an ice-cold rifle,
His aching jaws grip a hot parch'd tongue,
His wide eyes search unconsciously.
He cannot shriek.
Bloody saliva
Dribbles down his shapeless jacket.
I saw him stab
And stab again
A well-killed Boche.
This is the happy warrior,
This is he—

(Wordsworth's chivalric poem goes on "That every man in arms should wish to be.") Wordsworth wrote in a day when the poetry-writing classes were seldom identical with the war-fighting classes. The two came together in the Great War. The result was a number of highly literate young soldiers and officers equipped by talent and education and instructed by alarming experience to do severe rhetorical damage to the chivalric idea.

One of the most forceful, even if not one of the most subtle, was Siegfried Sassoon. The mystique of the *comitatus* could hardly survive his depiction of inept commanders in poems like "The General" or "Base Details," nor could the chivalric mystique of self-sacrifice for a quasi-Christian cause survive undamaged his poem "The One-Legged Man," where the demobilized veteran, delighted to have purchased his life with the loss of only one leg, hobbles cheerfully around his garden, thinking, "Thank God they had to amputate!" The chivalric conception of women does not come unscathed through Sassoon's sardonic assaults on it in "Glory of Women":

You love us when we're heroes, home on leave,
Or wounded in a mentionable place.
You worship decorations; you believe
That chivalry redeems the war's disgrace.
You make us shells. You listen with delight,
By tales of dirt and danger fondly thrilled.
You crown our distant ardors while we fight,
And mourn our laurelled memories when we're killed.
You can't believe that British troops "retire"
When hell's last horror breaks them, and they run,
Trampling the terrible corpses, blind with blood.
   O German mother dreaming by the fire,
     While you are knitting socks to send your son
     His face is trodden deeper in the mud.

There Sassoon quite unchivalrously damns rather than celebrates the wartime innocence (that is, ignorance) of women, and with that action (homosexually motivated as it doubtless is in his case) he signals what is virtually a new attitude.

To the traditional imagination in the late nineteenth century, it was taken for granted that one's attitude toward one's mother should be conspicuously chivalric, if not reverential. It was axiomatic not only that Mother Knows Best, but—more startling—that A Boy's Best Friend Is His Mother.

Wherever you went, Mother was likely to go too, safeguarding your chastity, making sure you were protected from the evils of drink and tobacco and low friendships. And from Mother's omnipresence you suffered no loss of manliness. When Douglas MacArthur arrived at West Point as a cadet in 1899, he was attended by Mother. She lived there for four years as self-appointed moral-tutor-in-residence, scrutinizing his every move, awarding praise or blame as appropriate. And when, commissioned a second lieutenant, he proceeded to his first post, in San Francisco with the Corps of Engineers, she accompanied him. In England at about the same time, Lord Northcliffe, the newspaper magnate, was revealing by his extravagant devotion to his mother how deeply he was dyed in the style of the period. His mother he always called "darling," while his wife was only "dear." On his deathbed, his last coherent words were, "Tell Mother she is the only one."

In such an atmosphere, it was to be expected that mothers would not just demand their due but would seize all the power they could grasp. Franklin D. Roosevelt's mother, Sara Delano Roosevelt, would be found, by any civilized standard, a terrible person. She was ignorant, intolerant, and opinionated, uneducated but assertive, anti-Semitic and snobbish, a lifetime practitioner of the *libido dominandi*, and she visited her tyranny on anyone she could cow. Her favorite victim was Franklin's wife, but Franklin himself was by no means safe from her bullying and nosiness. When he went to Harvard, she quite naturally moved into an apartment in Cambridge, where for the full four years she kept the customary motherly eye on him. She never willingly yielded her prerogatives to meddle and interfere. According to Ted Morgan, one of Roosevelt's biographers, Betsy Cushing, his daughter-in-law, was once in his office with him when the Secretary of State telephoned. As she remembers, Roosevelt picked up the phone and said, "Oh yes, Cordell."

> She pointed at herself and silently mouthed,
> "Shall I go?" and FDR shook his head. Then he
> said, "Mama, will you please get off the line—
> Mama, I can hear you breathing, will you *please*
> get off the line?"

You sometimes see a photograph of a sad-faced Roosevelt at his desk just after Pearl Harbor. He is signing the Congressional Declaration of War, and on his left jacket sleeve he wears a black mourning band. Captions on this picture sometimes assert that by this traditional token he is mourning the deaths of the 2,000 men killed on December 7, 1941. Not at all. He is mourning his mother, who died three months before. The erroneous caption measures the speed with which we have moved past the traditional usages, especially those associated with the overpowering devotion to Mother.

To realize the oddity of this canonization of Mother, the historian of ideas and styles must try to imagine it flourishing in the Renaissance or the eighteenth century. It clearly belongs only to the nineteenth and to its afterglow in the earlier part of the twentieth. Mother is "the noblest thing alive," says Coleridge in 1818. And once Victoria matured into motherhood, her image as patriotic totem and head of

THE FATE OF CHIVALRY—241

the Established Church doubtless added a weight more than trivially sentimental to the mother cult. It was during her reign that it became popular to domesticate Britannia, formerly imagined as a rather threatening classical warrior, by designating her "Mother Britain." (It is impossible today to envisage or delineate a noble allegorical Brittania. She has suffered a fate similar to the demeaning of the female "America" referred to in the GI graffito in the Saigon latrine: AMERICA LOST HER VIRGINITY IN VIETNAM, to which a later hand has added: YES, AND SHE CAUGHT THE CLAP TOO.)

And it was just after Victoria's reign that the mother fixation attained an additional ritualizing, at least in the United States, when in 1908 a new holiday, Mother's Day, was devised—by florists, the cynical said. This rapidly developed symbolic floral conventions, like sons wearing a white or red carnation to proclaim their homage to Mother whether dead or living.

The soldiers of 1914–1918 began the war with their traditional imaginations intact, and it seemed wholly appropriate that their main visitors at their training camps should be not girlfriends, mistresses, or even wives, but mothers. It is not surprising that a Civil War song was revived for this later occasion, a song requiring the singer to announce, "Just before the battle, Mother, I am thinking most of you." The prevailing Victorian attitudes toward Mother are readily available in a little book produced by the Rev. Dr. L. M. Zimmerman, the Methodist pastor of Christ Church, Baltimore, titled *Echoes from the Distant Battlefield* and issued in 1920. Zimmerman had corresponded copiously with his boy-soldier parishioners during the war, and in his book he selected highminded chivalric passages from their letters to him. Hardly a one neglects to deliver "period" encomiums to Mother. One soldier, commenting on the loneliness in camp on Sundays, says, "One longs to see . . . his best friend, his mother, God bless her." And introducing a letter from a hospitalized soldier, Zimmerman points out—the parallelism seems significant—that "His Mother and his God are his very first thoughts." Many of Zimmerman's correspondents emphasize that only the principles of chastity enjoined by Mother have kept them pure abroad, amid the numerous temptations incident to residence in Latin countries.

Indeed, the ultimate monitor and gauge of perfect purity is Mother. "Don't use language your mother would blush to hear," the American soldier is adjured by a YMCA pamphlet of 1918. And it is assumed as too obvious for discussion that the main sufferers in the war are by no means the soldiers in the cold and deadly line, but the mothers at home. Their *sacrifice*—the word was used freely—was recognized by the more traditionally minded of their sons as even greater than the one required of them. "GIVE YOUR SONS," commands one pre-conscription pamphlet issued by the British Mothers' Union. It goes on to invoke chivalric images, casting Mother now in the role formerly played by the knight's courtly mistress. "The right sort of Mother for Old England," says this pamphlet, must gird the armor on her son "just as truly as the ladies of old braced on the armor of their knights." And no one seemed to doubt a mother's ability to override her son's instinctive pacifism or her capacity to deliver him up to the services on call. One mother depicted on a U.S. Navy recruiting poster resolutely presents her boy to Uncle Sam with the words, "Here he is, Sir." Mother's coercive power is similarly recognized in a British recruiting leaflet shrewdly addressed not to sons but to their mothers: "MOTHERS!" this leaflet asserts, "One word from YOU and he will go." Likewise a British poster shows a white-haired mother with her hand on her son's shoulder. He looks uncertainly into the distance, but she gestures thitherward broadly, saying to him, "GO! IT'S YOUR DUTY, LAD. JOIN TODAY." Did the British recruiting slogan say, "Every single one is ready to carry a gun"? No, it said, "Every mother's son is ready to carry a gun."

The conservative poet Alfred Noyes, writing for the government on behalf of the war effort, visited a munitions factory in September 1916, as the gruesome Somme battle was beginning to wear itself out. In the armaments factories, Noyes insisted, there was no labor trouble whatever, as the troops frequently believed. Indeed, the affection of the workers (many of them women) for their work can be described only as motherly. The women Noyes saw working, he reports, as they heaved "great shells into the shaping machines" or pulled "red-hot copper bands from furnaces, . . . seemed to lavish all the passion of motherhood upon their work; for this gleaming brood of shells, rank after rank, had indeed been brought forth to shield a dearer brood of flesh and blood. 'Mothers of the Army' was the thought that came to one's mind. . . . An army of little mothers. . . ."

Like other tenets of the chivalric code, this mother cult is going to suffer grave wartime damage. Before the war, it would seem that the customary family quarrels popular in literature were with Father, Mother being protected by chi-

valric convention—privileged, as it were. In books like Samuel Butler's *The Way of All Flesh* (1903) and Edmund Gosse's
Father and Son (1907) Mother is still sacrosanct, and it is
Father who is exposed as an ignorant bully or a menace to
the freedom of the young. But after the shocks and disillu-
sionments of the Great War, satiric assaults upon Mother
begin to recommend themselves to the new postwar audience. And despite the formal persistence of Mother's Day,
the former adoration of Mother has scarcely weathered the
scorn of such psychically damaged veterans as Hemingway,
Remarque, and Graves.

Looking back over Hemingway's total production, one
notices that although there are some fathers in it, like "My
Old Man," mothers are virtually absent. Indeed, the Hemingway hero, like Jake Barnes or Frederic Henry, seems to
belong to no family at all. But on the one occasion when a
mother makes a conspicuous appearance in Hemingway's
writing she is ruthlessly anatomized and ridiculed. I have in
mind the short story "Soldier's Home," published in Paris in
1924 in the volume *In Our Time*. Here, Harold Krebs, a
Marine Corps corporal who has been through the bloodiest
battles on the Western Front, returns badly shaken to his
somnolent, incurious middle-western town. (Some have
identified it with Oak Park, Illinois, Hemingway's parents'
home.) The gulf is deep and unbridgeable between his empirical knowledge of the war and his mother's sentimental
image of it. For him, it has changed everything. For her, it
has changed nothing, since to her mind it has been only a
matter of received images and clichés, words about *gallantry*
and *little Belgium*. For her, we find, the war has meant pri-

marily a threat to Harold's chastity. She is disturbed now at his lassitude, his unwillingness to resume his prewar life as if nothing has happened:

"Have you decided what you are going to do yet, Harold?" his mother said, taking off her glasses.

"No," said Krebs.

"Don't you think it's about time?" . . .

"I hadn't thought about it," Krebs said.

"God has some work for everyone to do," his mother said. "There can be no idle hands in His Kingdom."

"I'm not in His Kingdom," Krebs said.

"We are all of us in His Kingdom."

Krebs felt embarrassed and resentful. . . .

"I've worried about you so much, Harold," his mother went on. "I know the temptations you must have been exposed to. I know how weak men are. . . ."

After exhorting Harold to make something of himself and become a credit to the community, his mother asks, "Don't you love your mother, dear boy?" In 1910 he would have answered, "Of course." Now he answers, "No." She collapses in tears, and he realizes that, having uttered the inexplicable postwar thing, he must make amends:

He went over and took hold of her arm. She was crying with her head in her hands.

"I didn't mean it," he said. "I was just angry at
something. I didn't mean I didn't love you."

He manages to pacify her, whereupon she says, "I'm your
mother. . . . I held you next to my heart when you were a
tiny baby." Before the war, this appeal might have reduced
Harold to a subservient atonement, but now, we are told,
"Krebs felt sick and vaguely nauseated." His mother invites
him to kneel and pray with her. He declines. As he leaves
the house he feels sorry for his mother, but he knows that
soon he will have to leave home for good.

Equally unable to understand the way the war has
changed everything for those who fought it is Paul Bäumer's
mother in Remarque's *All Quiet on the Western Front* (1929).
When Paul returns home on leave, he discovers that the only
way the new world of the trenches, that is, the new world
of industrialized mass violence, can greet the traditional one
is by lies. "Was it very bad out there, Paul?" his mother asks,
and, hating himself, he answers, "No, Mother, not so very."
And as he prepares to return to the front, she honors the
prewar convention that one of a mother's main duties is
preventing her son's access to sexual pleasure (or, once he is
married, hating the agent of it). She says: "I would like to
tell you to be on your guard against the women in France.
They are no good." And he informs her: "Where we are
there aren't any women, Mother." Formerly the all-wise
Boy's Best Friend, Mother has now turned into a hopelessly
unimaginative, ignorant, sentimental drone and parasite.

And there's a similar mother, but a more dangerous
one, in another important work of 1929, Graves's highly

fictionalized memoir *Good-bye to All That.* Here, the mother is a literary character devised by someone in the British propaganda services. He has denominated her "A Little Mother," and in a letter imputed to her, reprinted in a vastly popular pamphlet of 1916, she is made to reprehend any thought of a compromise peace by insisting that any such would be an insult to mothers who have already "sacrificed" their sons. Her bloodthirsty call for more war is accompanied by a train of solemn illiterate testimonials from third-rate newspapers, noncombatant soldiers, and fictional bereaved mothers, one of whom is quoted as saying: "I have lost my two dear boys, but since I was shown the 'Little Mother's' beautiful letter a resignation too perfect to describe has calmed all my aching sorrow, and I would now gladly give my sons twice over."

From these and similar exposures of maternal self-righteousness, callousness, and egotism the mother cult never recovered, and by the 1920s it was one of the numerous casualties of the Victorian understanding of human rights and privileges. The British infantry veteran Charles Carrington has described the way the war was recalled in the disillu-sioned memoirs and novels of the late 1920s: "Every battle a defeat, every officer a nincompoop, every soldier a coward." And, we can add, every mother a monster. Twenty more years would virtually complete the ruin of the chivalric mother, when, in 1942, Philip Wylie, in his wide-ranging satire *Generation of Vipers,* stigmatized Mom and Momism as central signs, if not causes, of cultural backwardness and perpetual psychological adolescence. And by the time of the film *Midnight Cowboy,* in 1969, the mere display of Mother's picture in an easel frame in a hotel room constitutes bad

news. To the village Freudians we have all become, it stigmatizes the elderly traveling businessman who solicits the
"cowboy" Joe Buck as a thoroughly pathetic and unsavory
type.

Thus the transition from the chivalric to the antichivalric, from romance to irony, or, as H. W. Massingham's *Nation*
put it as early as 1915, "The development of war from a
dilettante art into a national business, from armor and capar-
isons to khaki and cartridge belts." The whole process, relatively rapid as it has been, might be taken to be an image of
the much longer process of secularization since the Middle
Ages. In the spring of 1912, after the *Titanic* disaster, a
number of American women contributed money toward a
monument to be installed in Washington, D.C., a monument
specifically devoted "to the everlasting memory of male chivalry"—that is, the action of many gentlemen aboard the
Titanic in insisting that the women and children occupy the
lifeboats, leaving themselves to drown. "To the . . . *memory* of
male chivalry": there, even if unintentionally, is the appro-
priately elegiac note. Today it would be impossible to imagine
in a plane-crash-evacuation the men standing aside, calmly,
nobly inhaling flames and gases for several minutes and feeling their fingers, ears, and noses burning off, while encouraging the women and children to leave down the slides. Like
much else that is traditional, chivalry has proved unsuited to
the world we have chosen to create.

MODERNISM, ADVERSARY CULTURE, AND EDMUND BLUNDEN

"There are few mental exertions more instructive," says Coleridge, "than the attempt to establish and exemplify the distinct meaning of terms often confounded in common use and considered as mere synonyms." He proceeds to instance honorifics like *agreeable, beautiful, picturesque, grand,* and *sublime.* If he were here now, I think he might enjoy desynonymizing a couple of latter-day critical terms. I am thinking of the word Modernist as distinguished from the word Modern. If Coleridge could be present and rapidly brought up to date, he might approve a distinction between those two terms that would go like this. A Modernist is a late-nineteenth- or early-twentieth-century artist or artistic theorist who has decided to declare war on the received, the philistine, the bourgeois, the sentimental, and the democratic. Thus one early Modernist is the Oscar Wilde who makes an enemy of "realism," and a later one is Virginia Woolf thirty years after who declares that "we want to be rid of realism." Likewise, T. E. Hulme stigmatizes as the enemy the "vital"—that is, lifelike—literature and art of the nineteenth century, and urges that this vital tradition be ousted by the new geometrical (or as we should call it, abstract) art. If Wilde and Woolf and Hulme make an enemy of "realism," Joyce and D. H. Lawrence war with religion, family, and nation, not to mention the conventions of emotional, especially sexual, repression adhered to by their forefathers. The battles of T. S. Eliot were fought against the cult of romantic personality, and in the United States William Carlos Williams and E. E. Cummings conducted their warfare against canons of conventionality in poetic technique. Wyndham Lewis labored to extirpate the enemies he designated in *BLAST:* "BLAST humor—Quack English drug for stupidity and sleepiness. . . . BLAST sport. . . . BLAST years 1837 to 1900."

Having exemplified one meaning of the term Modernist, an up-to-date Coleridge would proceed to suggest the way an artist or critic fit to be called a Modern differs. A Modern, he might conclude, is capable of incorporating into his work contemporary currents of thought and emotion without any irritable need to quarrel with the past—intellectually, psychologically, or technically. A Modern can embrace the past and not just feel but enjoy its continuity with the present. As some exemplary Moderns I'm thinking of Edward Thomas, Robert Frost, Edwin Muir, Louis MacNeice, Conrad Aiken, and Elizabeth Bishop. Disdain for their literary forebears is not their stock in trade, and they can produce their art without strenuous adversary gestures toward either the past or a present which differs from them in some of its critical opinions. To illustrate: the further we move past W. H. Auden's moment, the more it becomes apparent that, in these terms, he was less a Modernist than a Modern, devoting himself largely to refining and complicating a received tradition, the tradition of Victorian light verse.

In a critical world dominated, as ours tends to be, by Modernist theory, the mere Moderns get systematically shortchanged, relegated to a position in the canon equivalent in the restaurant to the little table back near the kitchen door. Although spokesmen for the Modernist movement conceive its main enemy to be Romanticism, ironically its own roots, its emotional roots at any rate, are traceable directly to the Romantic Movement. The model world of adversary Modernism is, indeed, the melodrama of the French Revolution, and its portrait of the sentimental bourgeois enemy of art it derives from the Romantic socialism of the middle and later nineteenth century. The shrill adversary tonalities of actual revolutionary utterance echo in many Modernist manifestos intended to influence the public, and the same tone is audible even in Modernist private letters, a literary form normally the venue of courtesy and charm.

"The modern self," says Lionel Trilling (and he means in my terms the Modernist self), "is characterized by certain habits of indignant perception." D. H. Lawrence afire with self-righteous fury makes a good example. Writing to a friend about the current inhabitants of Taormina, he strikes a note suggestive either of Jacobin polemic or the aristocratic rejoinder to it. Taormina, he asserts, "is a world of *canaille:* absolutely. *Canaille, canaglia, Schweinhunderei,* stink-pots. Pfui!— pish, pshaw, prrr! They all stink in my nostrils. That's how I feel in Taormina . . . , that's how I feel. A curse, a murrain, a pox on this crawling, sniffling, spunkless brood of humanity." If we seem to catch there the rumbling of the tumbrils moving toward the scaffold, that sound is even louder and clearer in the utterances of Pound when he is at work opposing the practitioners of the genteel tradition in America. "I personally would not feel myself guilty of manslaughter," he says, "if by any miracle I ever had the pleasure of killing [Henry Seidel] Canby or the editor of the *Atlantic Monthly* and their replicas, and of ordering a wholesale death and/or deportation of a great number of affable, suave, moderate men, . . . all incapable of any twinge of conscience on account of any form of mental cowardice or any falsification of reports whatever." And in 1922, the year of such Modernist performances as *The Waste Land, Ulysses,* cummings's *The Enormous Room,* Williams's *Spring and All,* and Edith Sitwell's *Façade,* Pound was telling a professor who had remonstrated with him about the violence of his opposition to the tradition, "There are things I quite definitely want to destroy, and which I think will have to be annihilated before civilization can exist." Some of these menaces—they turn out to be human beings like writers, manufacturers, bankers, and churchmen—Pound consigns to his "Hell" Cantos, where he sets them to writhing in obscene postures.

Even the decorous T. S. Eliot can get off some pretty vigorous insults against such adversaries as journalistic reviewers, not-very-bright readers, literary snobs and name-droppers, posturing feeble poets, and late-Romantic artistic phonies. "If we attend to the confused cries of the newspaper critics and the *susurrus* of popular repetition that follows," Eliot writes, "we shall hear the names of poets in great numbers; if we seek not Blue-book knowledge but the enjoyment of poetry, and ask for a poem, we shall seldom find it." And when in "Tradition and the Individual Talent" he goes on to point out that, contrary to Romantic views about the sources of art in self-expression, poetry is actually an escape from the expression of emotion and personality, he adds the quiet but nevertheless devastating insult, "But of course only those who have personality and emotions know what it means to want to escape from these things." And it must be said that such an adversary stance would seem very tempting when, as Siegfried Sassoon recalls, someone like Edmund Gosse was describing Eliot as "an American poetaster . . . who has been making himself ridiculous by his condemnation of *Hamlet.*" Sassoon himself played at being a Modernist for a while before settling into his more instinctive role as a Modern. In 1921 he felt himself entirely estranged from the philistine world—represented, as so often with Modernists, by his mother. Her tastes ran to "G. F. Watts and holy communion," he noted, while his propelled him in quite the opposite direction, toward "Green Chartreuse and Epstein sculpture."

·　　·　　·　　·

For these self-conscious Modernists of the 1920s and 1930s, the new institution of the adversary culture could seem to acquire validation and authority from the shrewd criticism of José Ortega y Gasset, the distinguished Professor of Philosophy at the University of Madrid. If a decent, ordinary person, accustomed in the Victorian way to expect art somehow to refract his own life and the lives of his family and friends, happened into a bookshop in 1925 and picked up a volume titled *The Dehumanization of Art,* he would naturally expect to find an attack, and a most welcome one, on the new abstract painting, or on the levities of Dada, or on the willful obscurities of the new poetry. How shocked he would be to find, as find he would, that for Ortega, *Dehumanization* is a good thing, and that far from castigating the new art for its departures from apparent human norms (Picasso's women would be an example), he is celebrating it precisely for its deviations from the Victorians' kind of humanization.

The essential perception in Ortega's work is that the humanistic "realism" sought by nineteenth-century art and narrative constitutes not a perceptual norm but simply another style in the history of styles, a style devised in the nineteenth century to register something precious to it, just as the late Renaissance invented Baroque or the eighteenth century the Augustan style to do the same thing. Before the egalitarian nineteenth century, Ortega points out, artistic styles had been valued for their *deviation* from "real life," and thus he can say of the nineteenth century that "its products, far from representing a normal type of art, may be said to mark a maximum aberration in the history of taste." The inordinate expansion of egalitarian assumptions and thus the increase in mediocre, necessarily unsubtle public education have helped cause this deplorable situation, and now the new literal-minded middle classes naturally prefer the art of the waxworks to the arts of abstract design. As Pound puts it in *Mauberley,*

The "age demanded" chiefly a mould in plaster,
Made with no loss of time,
A prose kinema, not, not assuredly, alabaster
Or the "sculpture" of rhyme.

To Ortega and his followers, the taste of the nineteenth century has been simply a bizarre anomaly, for as he says,

All great periods of art have been careful not to let the work revolve about human contents. [Byzantium is perhaps the example he has in mind.] The imperative of unmitigated realism that dominated the artistic sensibility of the last century must be put down as a freak in aesthetic evolution.

It is possible, therefore, to consider Modernist "dehumanized" art not a divagation from but a return to what Ortega calls "the royal [that is, definitely not plebeian] road of art." This road he identifies with "the will to style," and he concludes that "to stylize means to deform reality, to derealize; style involves dehumanization." To express this another way, we can invoke Northrop Frye's distinction between the "low-mimetic" or eighteenth- and nineteenth-century ways of depicting characters and actions and the Modernist way, which he designates the Ironic. The difference is between, say, the artistic procedures of Trollope, on the one hand, and Samuel Beckett on the other.

But it is not merely Ortega's views on the old and the new styles that would delight the Modernist and puzzle or dismay the ordinary person. Even more inflammatory to the uninitiated would be the encouragement Ortega offers to the Modernist adversary impulse. Modern art, he declares, "will always have the masses against it," for it is not just unpopular: it is "anti-popular," dividing society into those who get it and those who don't. "Hence," Ortega says, "the indignation it arouses in the masses." Regarded politically, the Modernist movement, according to Ortega, is art's revenge for "a hundred years of adulation of the masses and apotheosis of the people."

One traditional genre of painting the new art makes impossible is sympathetic portraiture, which is incompatible with the revived emphasis on style, not representation, as the end of art. As Ortega emphasizes, "Preoccupation with the human content of the work is in principle incompatible with aesthetic enjoyment proper." It used to be different, he admits: "With the things represented on traditional paintings we could have imaginary intercourse. Many a young Englishman has fallen in love with Gioconda. With the objects of modern pictures no intercourse is possible." Or, to turn from painting to poetry, which of Eliot's characters could one fall in love with, sympathize much with, or even admire? Hardly Madame Sosostris, the late-drinking pub wives or the hysterical society woman, the passive Thames maidens, the sexually violated, unfeeling typist, the perverse Mr. Eugenides, the brutal Sweeney. In the same way, what response except satiric contempt seems called for by Pound's Mr. Nixon, or his Lady Valentine?

At the moment the severe dehumanization of art was being called for by Ortega, a twenty-nine-year-old British poet, gentle, shy, generous, enthusiastic, was living in Tokyo and trying to use art, and thought as well, as therapeutic procedures for regaining his humanity. He had been badly beaten up by the Great War—gassed, traumatized, brought near to total disillusion and despair. He confessed some difficulty understanding the apparent cosmic pessimism of both Eliot and Joyce since neither had experienced the trenches at firsthand. He had, and much of his later life he spent trying to make some sense of that appalling business. Indeed, from 1918 to the end of his life he preserved a view of actuality that can be called the gentle infantryman's (*gentle* to distinguish it from Robert Graves's very different, angrily adversary view). After his experience of the war Blunden knew that being scared to death most of the time is undignified and ultimately unmanning, that bullets and shell fragments hurt, that absurdity and unreason—in literary criticism and artistic rationalization as well as in life—will get you if you don't watch out, and that living in an adversary environment was something he'd had quite enough of.

He was born in London in 1896. His parents were school-teachers. They soon moved to a school in Yalding, Kent, where Edmund grew up in an atmosphere of literary high-mindedness and laid in a lifetime's images of hop gardens, oast houses, and benign brooks and streams. There would ultimately be nine children in the family and little money, but being from boyhood a most assiduous reader and writer, Edmund won a scholarship to Christ's Hospital. There he conceived a lasting enthusiasm for some writers who had been Bluecoat Boys a century earlier—Coleridge, Lamb, and Leigh Hunt. His Greek and Latin grew impressive enough to win him a scholarship at Queen's College, Oxford, and at this point he could look forward to a lovely life of lettered repose.

But before he could install himself in his Oxford college, Britain declared war on the Central Powers, and soon this quiet young poet and literary scholar found himself commissioned in the Royal Sussex Regiment, where his shyness won him the nickname Bunny but his bravery won him the Military Cross. Miraculously he survived two years at the front, perhaps because he was sent home a gas casualty before he could be killed. After the war he joined the writers living at Boar's Hill, Oxford, where in proximity to Robert Bridges such young poet-veterans assembled as Graves, Edgell Rickword, and Robert Nichols. By 1920 Blunden had abandoned Oxford for London and a life of high journalism, assisting J. Middleton Murry on *The Athenæum* and producing countless literary essays and reviews. In 1922, that Modernist *annus mirabilis,* Blunden made his own gentle bid for fame, a volume of poems titled *The Shepherd,* which won the Hawthornden Prize and brought its author a good deal of notice. In a poem like "The Pasture Pond" the careful reader could detect a sophisticated pastoralism comparable to Andrew Marvell's lurking behind a mock-simple surface comparable to Robert Frost's. The scene of Blunden's pasture pond is very different from the world of literary dispute, for

> Here's no malice that could wither
> Joy's blown flower, nor dare come hither;
> No hot hurry such as drives
> Men through their unsolaced lives;
> Here like bees I cannot fare
> A span but find some honey there.

And birds of different species and sizes find

> No cause . . . to grudge or brawl,
> For nature gives enough for all.

But, as Blunden indicates in a poem like "1916 Seen from 1921," his pastoralism is war-haunted, stained by remembered horror, and that is why it is complicated and unpatronizable, even, as we might say, *modern*. In the midst of the Forest of Arden it is impossible to forget Mametz Wood, or as Blunden puts it,

> The charred stub outspeaks the living tree.

And in another poem ("Third Ypres"), which seems only ironically present in a volume called *The Shepherd*, Blunden revisits the worst experience of his life, the hours during the Battle of Passchendaele when the pillboxes sheltering his battalion were pierced by German shells and very many men were killed and wounded, their bloody parts strewn about inside the concrete rooms. His desire to get away from that terrible scene made the word *Relief* an obsession then, but now, as he says,

> who with what command can now relieve
> The dead men from that chaos, or my soul?

Blunden proved so unable to put the war decently behind him that his colleagues on the *Athenæum* feared for his sanity, and they encouraged him to take a restful voyage to South America, which he wrote up charmingly in *The Bonadventure: A Random Journal of an Atlantic Holiday,* the sort of bright, youthful travel book many were to produce in the twenties and thirties. Without quite asserting of postwar England "I Hate It Here," as so many did, Blunden found himself not immune to the temptations of exile, but he avoided the extreme adversary stances of such exiles as James Joyce, Robert Graves, Norman Douglas, and D. H. Lawrence. He took off for Japan and spent the years from 1924 to 1927 teaching English at the Imperial University of Tokyo. It was there, in a setting of modest beauty and order, ceremony and delicacy, that he recalled his wartime experiences for *Undertones of War,* his classic memoir published in 1928.

Back in England, he wrote for *The Nation* for a time, but finding he needed a more stable profession than literary journalism, he became a Fellow and Tutor of Merton College, Oxford, where over the years his devoted students included both Northrop Frye and Keith Douglas. To his academic duties he added work for the *Times Literary Supplement,* ultimately joining the staff and, in the days when its reviews and essays were anonymous, writing more of each number than might seem possible. The approach of a new war depressed him immensely, but during it he kept busy teaching map-reading to cadets stationed at Oxford. All this time he was bringing out one book after another—biographies of Leigh Hunt and Shelley and Hardy, editions of Christopher Smart and John Clare and William Collins, critical studies of the essayists of the Romantic period. After the Second World War he quit England again for Japan, this time as Cultural Liaison Officer with the British Mission. In two years he traveled all over the country and gave some six hundred lectures on English literature. And for eleven years, from 1953 to 1964, he served as Professor of English at the University of Hong Kong, retiring finally to Suffolk to a well-earned rest disturbed only in 1966 by the small, uninvited controversy between Ancients and Moderns culminating in his defeat of Robert Lowell for the postion of Professor of Poetry at Oxford. He died in 1974 in the quiet English countryside he loved, but the flowers that covered his coffin were not English pastoral flowers—they were Flanders poppies.

One thing apparent throughout Blunden's life was his disinclination to engage in adversary utterance or persuasion, either to advance his critical views, to object publicly to those advanced by others, or to aggrandize his particular kind of poetry. A typical avoidance of the adversary posture was his attitude toward his presumed rival for the Oxford Professorship. After the voting, Blunden said: "I'm very grateful to Mr. Lowell for giving me an exciting time in Oxford." Now if that had been said by a congenital scrapper like Field Marshal Sir Bernard Law Montgomery, or by a professional controvertist like Norman Mailer, we would assume ironic intent. But not so with Blunden—he means precisely what his words say. And he goes on to speak of Lowell this way: "If he'd been here [for the election] we could have talked about it over a glass. We wouldn't come to blows." His fondness for the eighteenth-century poets took him to the ones the least argumentative, bellicose, or satiric. When he was in the trenches, he asked his mother to send him the works of James Thomson and William Shenstone, not, notably, the combative productions of the onetime Modernists Pope and Swift, not even the works of the sainted Samuel Johnson, whose willingness to object and oppose on any pretext Blunden cannot have found his most admirable trait. And when Graves brought out *Good-bye to All That* in 1929, Blunden found himself deeply pained by Graves's readiness at abuse and contempt. What he specified as Graves's "cold use and slaughter of others" constitutes, he says, "in some way a betrayal of the experience of the war, and of those who . . . died in it." And from his point of view he is quite right: Graves does despise the colonel he nicknames "Buzz Off" as heartily as Blunden admires his battalion commander, Colonel G. H. Harrison, who remained a friend for life and the topic of more than one of Blunden's celebratory poems. With Graves's satiric view of most of his army colleagues and

subordinates we can contrast Blunden's lifelong admiration
for his sergeant, Frank Worley, also remembered in Blunden's poems. In the same way Blunden was always loyal
to his old school, in a way one can't imagine Graves
being toward Charterhouse, and certainly in a way one
can't possibly conceive Ezra Pound being toward *his* school
or university. Pound after all in later life wrote back
to his professor that the only thing the university would
do for a person of original intellect was to tell him to go
away.

If a way to establish one's identity as a Modernist is to
quarrel with one's predecessors, as if to suggest that the new
or current literary mode has finally located for all time the
permanent forms of verbal validity, Blunden is only a Modern. His feeling of indebtedness to the literary past is as lively
as his feeling for the social-historical past, as he develops it
in a poem like "Forefathers." In his sonnet "Victorians" he
quietly advises the current enemies of the preceding generation to read them first, and then to

Devise some creed, and live it, beyond theirs,
Or I shall think you but their spendthrift heirs.

It is always well for the reviler of the past to keep in mind,
as Blunden suggests in some characteristic lines titled "On
Tearing Up a Cynical Poem," that he himself will be, in his
turn, revileable. Always devoted to sport—cricket especially
—he deplored the increasing hostility attending athletic
events in the Modernist era, just as he deplored the hostilities

of literary history. Formerly, he notes in his poem "An International Football Match,"

> The other player, it was understood,
> Was as yourself, however went the day.

But now, how things have changed:

>   each snarling retrograde
> Prepares his malice for the coming guest,

and

> Men cannot shoot a goal or jump a hurdle
> Without a psychologic gas attack.

To Blunden, both sport and literature should be rather inclusive than divisive, and as Thomas Mallon writes, Blunden's literary-historical ideal is "a quiet community of poet, reader, *and past poet,*" that is, the other poet present in every poem by allusion, or present in a way (to the fully literate reader) even by absence.

Given this instinct for peace and quiet, one might expect Blunden to be but a feeble critic. Kenneth Hopkins, in fact, is largely right to say that "In all his critical writings, I do not think Blunden ever attacks or condemns anyone." Perhaps not, but he can be vigorously discriminating, as he is in his book on Hardy for the English Men of Letters Series. There he will surprise readers who imagine him nothing but a marshmallow by his unrelenting insistence that Hardy can sometimes write very bad poems, being only too liable, as Blunden notes, to "drag into metrical form" certain beloved "drifting commonplaces," or to invite into poems events which recommend themselves only by being literally and historically true. Indeed, Hardy's *Collected Poems,* at their worst "monotonous" and "dull," need to be cut to a fifth— no, a *tenth*—of their number. What misleads some readers into regarding Blunden's criticism as wholly appreciative and celebratory is his courteous manner and the modesty of his means, as in the Preface to his study of Hardy, where his addiction to the passive voice suggests a thorough Milque-toast rather than a strong discriminator. He writes: "In these pages some account of Hardy's life is given," and "A personal impression of his nature and his writings is attempted." In daily life, for all his gentleness Blunden could be mighty hardheaded and businesslike when required, not at all the dreamy pastoral poeticizer of popular imagery. In 1941, for example, when Keith Douglas, away in the army, was sending poems back to his mother to pass to Blunden to send to magazines, Blunden tells Mrs. Douglas that she must put the publication of the poems "on a business footing," which means that she should be sure that Keith "retain[s] the rights in the poems."

Thus, a context for Blunden. Now one should ask the question, What kind of writer is he? What is the worth of his work? Is he really Modern, and does it matter?

To begin with the bad news first. Some of his odd and self-indulgent rhetorical habits may suggest that he has become stuck somewhere back in the middle of the nineteenth century. Like his fondness for beginning a poem with an earnest apostrophe, often accompanied by the interjection "O!" Or his adhesion to the subjunctive mode when most other poets gave it up generations ago. Or his weakness for inverted word order. Or his addiction to quaint or archaic diction, like *whence* and *thence,* not to mention his calling poetry *verses,* prosody *verse-music,* and a book of poems a *poetry-book,* as well as referring to writers as *scribes*—sometimes *quillmen*—and calling writing itself, on one occasion, *pencraft.* And what about his genteel expletives, like "Bless me!" or "As I live"? If those things can be overlooked, how about his use of exclamation marks in his poems, or his ripe and chummy way of referring to the Great of the past with the word *old* as in Old Chaucer or Old Camden?

And there are other characteristics, of theme and focus as well as style, that may put off the devotee of Modernist—and sometimes even of Modern—writing. Like Blunden's unabashed patriotism, for example. Or his not scrupling to produce poems for specific occasions. Or his speaking right out in his own undisguised person, his "I" not for a moment pretending to stand for J. Alfred Prufrock or Sextus Propertius, and speaking out personally to memorialize some moment in his own life. All such behavior is likely to offend the reader nurtured on the Modernist classics and tempt him to dismiss Blunden as a mere late-Romantic pastoral-minded reactionary.

But wait. When we read his poems carefully, we notice something unexpected, and then we may want to agree with what H. M. Tomlinson says of *Undertones of War:* "The poet's eye," he notes, "is not in a fine frenzy rolling," and he continues: "There is a steely glitter in it." The steely glitter is often there in Blunden's poems too, and it arises from their frequent enactment of an ironic dynamics—soothingly led to expect mere "charm," we are brought, instead, to scandal. His poems have the effect of shaking us out of the complacency to which they seem to invite us. For example. A standard kind of poem from the Great War is one which finds an odd beauty in the trench scene. This poem deploys an optimistic or romance "plot": it first projects the normal materials of ugliness and seems to invite the normal response, and then it pretends to read them more intensely and contemplate them more sensitively and thus discover the beauty that was there all the time. This is what Richard Aldington's poem titled "Soliloquy #2" does. It depicts the "shattered trenches" after an attack has passed over them and describes

> lying upon the fire-step,
> A dead English soldier,
> His head bloodily bandaged
> And his closed left hand touching the earth.

But as the poem moves through its final four lines, out of this cadaver is born an almost redeeming beauty. "More beautiful than one can tell," the poem goes on,

> More subtly coloured than a perfect Goya,
> And more austere and lovely in repose
> Than Angelo's hand could ever carve in stone.

Blunden's way, on the contrary, is quietly to astonish the reader by reversing the normal procedure, as he does in his fifteen-line poem "Illusions." The beauty comes first, then the destruction, or rather the complication, of that illusion. But there are really three phases in the poem through which the understanding passes: first the illusion of beauty; then the illusion of menace, generated by corpse-rags fluttering on the barbed wire; then finally the dissipation of the illusion of menace into an illusion of quiet, ironic horror. Here is the poem:

Trenches in the moonlight, in the lulling moonlight
Have had their loveliness; when dancing dewy grasses
Caressed us passing along their earthly lanes;
When the crucifix hanging over was strangely
    illumined,
And one imagined music, one even heard the brave bird
In the sighing orchards flute above the weedy well.
There are such moments; forgive me that I note them,
Nor gloze that there comes soon the nemesis of beauty,
In the fluttering relics that at first glimmer wakened
Terror—the no-man's ditch suddenly forking:
There, the enemy's best with bombs and brains and
    courage!
—Softly, swiftly, at once be animal and angel—
But O no, no, they're Death's malkins dangling in the
    wire
    For the moon's interpretation.

That's a characteristic Blunden poem: we think we know where we are, and we become comfortable with the tone and movement, and then we learn that we've not known all the time what we might have known. The structure of "Illusions" is like that of the poem "Concert Party: Busseboum," where the first half conducts us into the delight of a soldier show behind the lines, full of laughter and singing, but the second half, depicting the audience leaving, dispels the illusion that in such a world escape from horror is possible, for now

> We heard another matinee,
>   We heard the maniac blast
>
> Of barrage south by Saint Eloi. . . .
>
> To this new concert, white we stood;
>   Cold certainty held our breath;
> While men in the tunnels below Larch Wood
>   Were kicking men to death.

The effect is like discovering in the midst of a pastoral field a snake in the grass, and that effect is possible only if you know how to entice the reader joyfully into the pastoral field in the first place. Or into a scene of homely recreation—ice skating this time—as in "The Midnight Skaters," where it is precisely the fun that betrays the presence of the menace.

> Can malice live in natural forms,
>   As tree, or stone, or winding lane?

he asks in the poem "The Ballast-Hole," which goes on to answer the question:

> Beside this winding lane of ours
> The fangy roots of trees contain
> A pond that seems to feed the powers
> Of ugly passion. Thunder-storms
> No blacker look. If forth it shook
> Blue snarling flashes lightning-like
> I scarce should marvel; may it strike
> When I'm not by its sullen dyke!

That is like Frost's "Design," or his "Tree at My Window," or his "Desert Places," which it resembles by shrewdly couching its highly pessimistic, hence "Modern" attitude in a mode which is not at all Modernist.

A similar complicated and not-at-all complacent poem of Blunden's is "Sheet Lightning," a poem which seems not very well known or often anthologized because presumably untypical of the sweet and pastoral Edmund Blunden. Here a group of men returning from a village game feel themselves sobered to an unaccustomed solemnity by a sudden outbreak of sheet lightning, whereupon

> each man felt the grim
> Destiny of the hour speaking through him.

But by the time they reach a wayside pub, fright and seriousness are forgotten, and the ribaldry resumes—and the petty abuse and cruelty and "anger's balefire." And as the group finally boards the brake again to leave,

> The waiting driver stooped with oath to find
> A young jack rabbit in the roadway, blind
> Or dazzled by the lamps, as stiff as steel
> With fear. Joe beat its brain out on the wheel.

That could be proposed as an eminently Modern poem, but probably it can't qualify as a Modernist one, for it renders the complicated modern scene in such a way as to engage human sympathy. Indeed, it would seem his fondness for people, with all their frailties and deformities, that finally helps Blunden not become a Modernist.

If the Modernist dehumanization of art has required the severe demotion if not the total disappearance of the portrait as a serious genre of painting, Blunden's art engages boldly with the kind of poem analogous to that sort of painting. I am thinking not just of his portraits of Colonel Harrison and Sergeant Worley, but also of the poem "Almswomen." There it is the George Crabbe of *The Borough* who is invited to join poet and reader in understanding and valuing the "two old dames" who live together in the village almshouse, proud of the show their garden makes from the road, praying amid tears "That both be summoned on the selfsame day." Imagine an Eliot or a Pound, not to mention a Wyndham Lewis, giving a damn about such people. Or about the couple of unprepossessing unfortunates Blunden depicts in "Lonely Love":

> Two walking—from what cruel show escaped?
> Deformity, defect of mind their portion,

and yet clearly in love, "She with her arm in his," causing
Blunden to pray,

> let her never have cause
> To live outside her dream, nor unadore
> This underling in body, mind and type. . . .

To try imagining such a topic as material for a confirmed
Modernist is to realize how deeply the Modernist movement
has been based on a satiric perception of contemporary actuality, where positive human values enter works of art only
by ironic negatives, like the exposure of modern love as only
rape or perversion in *The Waste Land.*

King Edward VIII's apostasy occurred over fifty years
ago, and doubtless some more years will pass before we will
learn from his edited letters what Eliot, for one, thought of
that event. But I think we can sense that Eliot would be
unlikely to defend Edward, and even more, to defend him on
the grounds that he was a lover, and a lover in a context of
cold British respectability. Blunden did defend him on those
grounds, in his "Verses to H. R. H. The Duke of Windsor,"
where Blunden observes

> That love should be shut out and hated
> By sound success cautiously mated

Indeed in England is not news;
Lovelessness will claim its dues.

Artistic Modernism has enjoyed such a favorable press for
the past eighty years or so that perhaps we've not sufficiently
noticed what we sense when we focus on a writer like
Blunden—namely, Modernism's limitations, its rejections
and refusals, its narrowness and exclusions, its emotional
chill, its dogmatisms refuted hourly by our own honest feelings. Would it be going too far to consider what Modernism
derived from the European political atmosphere of its time
(I am thinking both of Russia in 1917 and Germany in 1933)
as a way of suggesting that Modernism in its way is an artistic
refraction of totalitarianism? At any rate, a consideration of
Blunden's place in the literary scheme of things can also
trigger the question, What place are we to find in the canon
for those modern writers who either work in relatively dis-
valued genres—the memoir, like Peter Quennell and Christopher Isherwood; the essay, like Cyril Connolly and George
Orwell; the travel book, like Robert Byron and Peter Fleming
—or who, without specifically rejecting the thematic and
stylistic urges of the Modernists, pursue a way which does
not make an enemy of the usages of the past?

Blunden remains one of the neglected, an irony, considering
how much of his effort he devoted to resuscitating the neglected of the past—Lamb, Leigh Hunt, Clare, Smart, Collins, Kirke White, as well as the more recent neglected like
Ivor Gurney. But to revisit Blunden is to realize how much
life there is in even the neglected. To revisit Blunden is also

to be reminded of the basis of literary criticism and literary response in humanity rather than in any form of science, or pseudo-science. As Blunden says when writing of Kirke White, "In almost all our critical performances the affections play some part, and I do not see that anything can be done to keep them out." The only way they can be kept out is for critics to turn from the humane and the empirical and the difficult to the doctrinaire and the facile.

INDY

Nineteen eighty-two was a bad year for motor racing. Making a practice run at the Indianapolis Motor Speedway, driver Gordon Smiley was killed, just a week after driver Gilles Villeneuve was killed in Belgium. These two horrors let loose a cascade of objections to motor racing, most of them based on the assumption that human beings are rational creatures, despite the evidence to the contrary that was pouring in from the South Atlantic, where in the Falkland

Islands Argentinians and British were shooting and shelling each other to death over matters of national pride and publicity. While that mass murder was in progress, some journalists chose to find auto racing a scandal. In *Time* magazine, Tom Callahan deplored the whole enterprise of the Indianapolis 500: "Some 450,000 people," he wrote, "will perch or picnic at the Speedway on Sunday. Nobody knows how many of them are ghouls spreading their blankets beside a bad intersection." This reprehension of ghoulishness was attended by four gruesome color photographs of Smiley's bloody accident designed to gratify the ghoul in all readers. At the same time, Frank Deford was setting off his anti-Indy blast in *Sports Illustrated,* finding the race not a sport but a mere hustling of automotive products ("The drivers at Indy look much less like athletes than like a lot of congested billboards"). He concluded that among the spectators lurk a significant number of "barbarians." George Vecsey, in the sports pages of *The New York Times,* suggested that the Indy race is becoming too dangerous to be regarded as a sport. "I can see accidents," he said, "on the Long Island Expressway."

Were these people right? Is the Indy 500 a sporting event, or is it something else? And if something else, is it evil or benign? I went there to find out.

Although the automotive industry moved to Detroit early in this century, Indianapolis is still a motor city, swarming with car washes and auto-parts stores, and the sign on the road into town from the airport, WELCOME TO INDIANAPOLIS: CROSSROADS OF AMERICA, seems to imply that you're entering a place best reached by car. Here, nobody walks. One day I walked two and a half miles along Sixteenth Street to the Speedway, and in that one hour found myself literally the only person not in an automobile. Returning a few hours later, I was still the only walker, with the exception of a man who accosted me and tried to borrow sixty-two cents.

To a Northeasterner, Indianapolis seems at first a strangely retrograde repository of piety and patriotism. When I arrived, an editorial in the only paper in town was raising a populist voice in a call for school prayer, and a front-page box offered "Today's Prayer" just above "Today's Chuckle." After a short sojourn in Indianapolis one is no longer surprised at the imperious sign in the store window, GO TO CHURCH SUNDAY. Catholics wishing to arrive at the 500-mile race very early Sunday morning, like everyone else, have their needs cared for by the Archdiocese of Indianapolis, which has ruled that the race-going faithful may fulfill their holy Sunday obligation "by attending Mass the evening before." Indianapolis seems the sort of place where the President expects no one to guffaw or shout, "Oh, come off it!" when he asserts that someone or something is "in my prayers." In fact, the President would love Indianapolis. Driving to the Speedway, the motorist passes a billboard advertising (of course) cars, but bellowing also GOD BLESS AMERICA. At the Speedway, even at qualifying trials weeks before the race, the national anthem is played at every opportunity, and the official program carries odd vainglorious ads like one inserted by the International Association of Machinists and Aerospace Workers: "PRIDE—Pride helped build America into the greatest nation on earth."

"Naptown" is what many locals call Indianapolis, and

it does seem a somnolent place. Although it's a city and not a town, it's hard not to think of the Hoosier Booth Tarkington and those long, warm, sleepy afternoons when Penrod and Sam found nothing whatever to do. As I experienced the slowness of the Indianapolis pace—every transaction seems to drag on interminably, every delay is welcomed with friendly patience—I began to wonder whether speed and danger were not celebrated there one day a year just for the sheer relief and novelty of it, life being, on all other days, so safe, slow, and predictable. But friendly as well, it must be said. An elderly man flushing the urinal next to mine at the Speedway Motel, astonished at the noisy vigor of the flush, turned to me and although we'd not been introduced, kindly made me the audience for his observation, "Gawd, the *suction* on that son of a bitch! If you dropped it *in* there, you'd really lose it!" Ron Dorson, an authority on the anthropology of Indy, observes that although "in most public social settings . . . it is considered socially deviant for strangers to approach one another," at the Speedway things are different. There, "it becomes perfectly acceptable to engage total strangers in conversation about lap times, automotive technology, Speedway management, or race-driver intrigue." Something of pioneer individualism seems to linger in this friendliness, and on race Sunday, when you behold the infield crowded with campers, tents, trailers, and R.V.s, their occupants cooking and drawing water and cosseting children and making love in the friendliest fashion, you realize what the Indy setting really is. It's an early-nineteenth-century American pioneer campsite surrounded, as if fortuitously, by an early-twentieth-century two-and-a-half-mile track. And you almost begin to wonder if it's not the camping out, that primeval American ceremony of innocence, rather than the race and its excitements and hazards, that has drawn these multitudes here.

I'd say the people can be divided into three social classes: the middles, who on race day, in homage to the checkered flag, tend to dress all in black and white and who sit in reserved seats; the high proles, who watch standing or lolling in the infield, especially at the turns, "where the action is"; and the uglies, the overadvertised, black-leathered, beer-sodden, pot-headed occupiers of that muddy stretch of ground in the infield at the first turn known as the Snake Pit. These are the ones who, when girls approach, spiritlessly hold up signs reading SHOW US YOUR TITS. These uglies are sometimes taken to be the essence of Indy, and they are those Frank Deford probably has in mind when he speaks of "barbarians." But they are not the significant Indy audience. The middle class is—all those nice unstrenuous types arriving at the Speedway in cars bearing Purdue and Indiana State stickers.

The middles are privileged to participate in an exclusive social event, the classy pit promenade. Beginning three hours before the start, anyone who can wangle a pit pass strolls slowly up and down in the space between the pits and the track proper, all dressed up and watched enviously—that is the hope, at least—by the tens of thousands of social inferiors confined to the stands. On race morning in Indianapolis this is the stylish place to be, a place where one wouldn't dare show oneself unshaven or in dirty clothes. Many spandy-clean black-and-white getups are to be seen there, including trousers with two-inch black-and-white squares. Even though the social tone is compromised a bit by the presence of journalistic onlookers (that's how I got there), the thing struck me as comparable with some of the great snob social operations of the world, like appearing in or near the royal box at Ascot or visibly sipping champagne while watching the cricket at Lord's or even nodding slightly to well-dressed friends while ambling slowly down the Champs Élysées. But this Indy promenade is distinctly for middle-class people. The upper-middle class is not to be found at Indy. If you're the sort of person drawn to the U.S. Open or the America's Cup races at Newport, you're not likely to be seen at the Speedway.

From the outset, devotees of motor racing have felt anxieties about its place on the class-status ladder. Is motor racing on a par with cockfighting and female mud wrestling, or is it up there with pro football and even, perhaps, tennis? The surprise registered by an Indianapolis paper after the race in 1912 speaks volumes, socially: "There has been no better-mannered gathering in Indianapolis. . . . There was no pushing, no crowding, no profanity, no discourtesies." When the Chief Steward issues his portentous injunction, "Gentlemen, start your engines," we may feel that the first word insists a bit too much. Presumably, if women drivers were to become a regular feature at Indy, the formula would have to include "Ladies and . . . ," which some might think a further advance toward gentility. Janet Guthrie, who has so far been the only woman to participate (three times), says: "I think that racing's image needs all the help it can get. It has traditionally been a lowbrow image." Before being killed in the Austrian Grand Prix in 1975, Mark Donohue, who had graduated not just from college but from Brown, raced at Indy and sensed what an anomaly he was there. "I was considered different from the other Indy drivers," he said. "I had gone to college, I was articulate, and I didn't swear a lot."

The sense that racing will naturally sink proleward unless rigorously disciplined is what one takes away from a reading of the rule book promulgated by the United States Auto Club, the official supervisor of Indy racing. Cars are not to bear "undignified names," "improper language or conduct" is forbidden, and everything must be neat and clean at all times, just as a gentleman would wish: "*Appearance:* cars, crews, and all pit personnel whose appearance detracts from the character of the program may be excluded." (What's that aimed at, long hair? Terrible acne? Effeminate gestures?)

A similar aspiration to respectability seems partially responsible for the euphemisms that abound at Indy. Just as the self-conscious middle class may remark that someone has passed away (sometimes *over*), the Indy public-address announcer will inform the spectators that "We have a fatality." Instead of saying that there's been a terrible smash-up on the third turn, he'll say, "We have a yellow light." A car never hits the wall, it "gets into" it, or even "kisses" it. When a hurtling car comes into contact with the concrete wall, the driver may be said to have "visited cement city." Driver Danny Ongais, badly injured in a crash in 1981, spoke of it later not as the crash or even the accident but as "the incident." Everywhere there is the gentleman's feeling that if you pretend something has not happened, it has not. Thus the rule prohibiting cars from adding oil during the race. Adding oil would publicly acknowledge, as racing journalist Terry Reed points out, "that a car is blowing (or leaking) its original supply on the track, making the course even more hazardous." Almost immediately after Gordon Smiley's car and body nauseatingly stained the wall, it was repainted, white and pure. After that his tire marks on the third turn ran oddly into an immaculate expanse of white.

As Danny Ongais's indirection suggests, there are psychological as well as social reasons for all this euphemism. Racing is now deadly dangerous, with speeds over 200 miles an hour the rule. That makes more true than ever Jackie Stewart's point: "Motor racing will always be dangerous because you are always going too fast for things around you." Johnny Rutherford adds: "Very few drivers—maybe only a handful—are capable of running two hundred miles an hour." An example of one guy who wasn't, some say in Indianapolis, was the late Gordon Smiley. At least that's the way they rationalize in order to admit to no defect in the conditions, only in the weaker aspirants, thus making racing seem a wholesome and natural illustration of Darwinian selection. A pervasive atmosphere of risk shrouds a top driver's professional life. In June 1970, Jackie Stewart had occasion to realize that in the past months he'd "seen more of life and death than most people see in two lifetimes. Four weeks after Jimmy died, it was Mike Spence at Indianapolis; four weeks later, another friend, Ludovico Scarfiotti; four weeks more, to the day, it was Jo Schlesser in Rouen; and two weeks ago, Bruce McLaren at Goodwood. Now it's Piers. It just keeps on." The U.S.A.C. rule book says explicitly that "Automobile racing is a hazardous undertaking," and it implies it all the way through as when it notes that all drivers are required to remove dentures before starting or when it lays down precise specifications for easily detached steering wheels, "to aid in removing injured drivers from cars."

I have been really scared quite a bit, most notably in the infantry in the Second World War, when shells whined closer and closer and I waited for the final one to tear me to pieces. But I had another moment of sheer terror on May 22, 1982, at eleven in the morning, on the third day of qualifying at Indy, when I entered the Speedway through an underpass running beneath the track itself and for the first time heard those cars screaming by just overhead. They give off not just an almost unbearable sudden noise, but shocking heat and concussion as well. In their appalling *whoosh* is the quintessential menace of the Machine. Not even an observer feels entirely safe at the Speedway, and indeed the spectators are in actual danger all the time—from hurtling machines, tires, and fragments, and from the deadly methanol fuel, which burns with a scarcely visible flame, consuming ears and noses and fingers before onlookers are even aware that the victim is on fire. No wonder "13" is, by U.S.A.C. edict, never used in car numbering.

No wonder, either, that the rituals of the Indy world are so strenuously male, macho as all get-out. Women, even wives and girlfriends, weren't allowed in the pits until 1970. In 1976 Janet Guthrie, intent on breaking the male barrier for the first time, couldn't get her car to go fast enough to qualify for a starting position, but on her way to her car to try, as the journalist Dan Gerber remembers,

she is stopped by two slightly beer-crazed twenty-year-olds.

"Hey, Janet," one of them calls, "You gonna qualify?"

"I hope so," she replies, smiling, perhaps a little nervously.

"Well, we don't," the other boy calls back to her. "We hope you crash and burn where we can see you."

Actually, to understand just how male Indy is, you have only to scrutinize the famous Borg-Warner trophy, awarded annually to the winner after he has drunk from the traditional quart bottle of milk—not carton, bottle, for this is Indy which, except for speed, has made very few concessions to the modern world. On top of the Borg-Warner trophy is a silver male figure ten inches tall, signaling the finish of a race by vigorously deploying a checkered flag, despite the curious fact that he's quite naked and exhibiting a complete set of realistic male genitals, instead of what we might expect of Indiana, a cache-sexe, consisting maybe of a windblown bit of fabric. There he stands, quite immodestly undraped—unlike, say, the modest figure in front of Rockefeller Center—proclaiming for all to see the ideal maleness toward which Indy aspires.

The ideal whiteness too. Indy, as Ron Dorson says, is "a show staged by white people for a white audience." Blacks

are so rare among the spectators that you notice them specifically, and of course there are no black drivers, nor threat of any. (There was once a Jewish driver, Mauri Rose, but that's another story.) At a local cocktail party I broached the black topic as politely as I could and was told by one woman that blacks abjured the race because you had to sit for hours in the hot sun and, as is well known, blacks can't bear to sit

in the sun. Phoned for his views, the local NAACP spokesman fulminated, asserting that the situation is a scandal but
that all black representations had been ineffective. Once Indy
is over and the Speedway emptied for another year, you see
a lot of blacks there working for a week to sweep up the six
million pounds of litter the crowd leaves (together with odd
left-behinds like sets of teeth, and each time, two or three
quite decent cars inexplicably abandoned forever in the infield).

The combined weight of the litter suggests the size of
the crowd, estimated (the Speedway declines to issue a precise count) at around 400,000. That's half the total population of the state of Montana. And the size of the crowd
suggests another thing that's being celebrated beside speed.
A name for it would be gigantism. Indy is the biggest of
everything, "the largest single-day sporting event in the
world," as local publicity says, and as Roger Penske adds, for
the drivers it's "the biggest race in the world to win"; both
the purse and the publicity are the largest. There is more
press coverage—over 4,000 media people are there—than
of any similar event. So gigantic is the track that a spectator
sees only a tiny segment of it. Thus the public-address announcer is indispensable, performing over (naturally) "the
world's largest public-address system" to tell you what you
are missing. This means that every event is mediated through
language: "We have a yellow light." The Indy public-address
and radio announcers have always become public personages,
even stars, and young Paul Page, who recently succeeded Sid
Collins as the radio "Voice of the Indianapolis Five
Hundred," is as famous there as, say, Alistair Cooke is elsewhere.

It's not just the announcing that makes Indy so curiously a language event. It's the advertising, the sight of grown men proud to be walking around in caps that say VALVOLINE or GOODYEAR. The cars themselves, plastered with decals (CHAMPION, DIEHARD, STP), have been called "the world's fastest billboards." So precise are the contracts between advertisers and drivers that drivers are allowed to appear bareheaded only for the brief moment between removing the helmet and clapping on the required prole-cap, reading DOMINO'S PIZZA or QUAKER STATE. Officially, Indy is a celebration of "progress" in the motor-car and rubber-tire industries (the tires are supplied gratis by Goodyear). It's supposed to be a testing ground for improvements destined to make their way into your passenger car. But unofficially, it's a celebration of the charm of brand names, a recognition of their totemic power to confer distinction on those who wear, utter, or display them—and secondary distinction on those in the stands who recognize and respond to them. You achieve vicarious power by wearing the right T-shirt or cap and thus allying yourself with successful enterprises like BUDWEISER or GATORADE. By this display of "legible clothing," as Alison Lurie calls it, you fuse your private identity with external commercial success, redeeming your insignificance and becoming, for the moment, somebody. (A cruel and ironic end for Whitman's highly American awareness of the Self and the Other.) Even the lucky wearers of the coveted pit passes are vouchsafed this feeling of power, for the badges, not content to be merely what they are, are also little ads—for CHEVROLET CAMARO, the year I was there. A person unable to read (a real "barbarian," maybe) would get very little out of Indy.

. . . .

Obviously there's much more going on here than is commonly imagined by what Naptowners are likely to refer to as "the eastern press," and there's certainly more going on than an overpowering desire to see someone killed. There is a powerful and in my view benign element of ritual purgation about Indy, and the things purged are precisely such impurities as greed, vulgarity, snobbery, and sadism.

The events just before the race, presented always in the same order and with the same deliberate, ample timing, are enough to hint at this ritual element. It is a Sunday morning, a time once appropriate for other rituals of purgation. When I inquired why the race was held on Sunday despite protests from the local Baptists about profaning the Sabbath and the inconvenience of closed liquor stores, I was told that Monday, the holiday, was always available as a rain date. But the race seems to gravitate to a Sunday for deeper reasons.

We've entered the Speedway very early, at 7:00 or 8:00 in the morning, although the crazies will have poured in, already blotto on beer and clad in T-shirts proclaiming the wearer TOO DRUNK TO FUCK, when the gates open at 5:00. We're all anticipating the hour of start, 11:00, the hour when church services traditionally begin. By 9:30 virtually everyone involved in the unvarying pre-start ceremonies is in place. At 9:45, as—I'm quoting the official program—"the Purdue University Band plays 'On the Banks of the Wabash,' " the race cars, still inert, silent, dead things, a threat to no one, are pushed by hand from the pits to their starting positions on the too narrow track, where they are formed up into the eleven rows of a viciously hazardous but thoroughly traditional three-abreast arrangement. At 10:34 the Chief Steward makes a stately ritual circuit in the pace car, officially inspecting the track for impurities one last time. At 10:44, all rise: "The Star-Spangled Banner." At 10:47, heads bowed for the invocation, delivered by a local divine, who prays for a safe race and reminds us of the dead of all our wars—and all past Indys. One minute later, "Taps." It is Memorial Day, you suddenly remember. Two minutes after "Taps," the band plays, very slowly, "Back Home in Indiana." By this time I find that I am crying, for me always an empirical indication, experienced at scores of weddings and commencements, that I am taking part in a ritual. By the time the portentous voice issued its command to the gentlemen, I was ready to be borne out on a litter. And the race hadn't even started yet.

If, while witnessing these things, you come to understand that Indy has something more to do with Memorial Day than coincidence, you also realize that there's some ritual meaning in the event's occurring at the moment recognized as the division between spring and summer. For Dan Gerber, listening as a boy annually to the Voice of the Indianapolis Five Hundred meant—release. "It meant school was getting out and I could get sunburned and go fishing and spend three months on Lake Michigan." It has meant something similar to me: the university year has ended, grades have been turned in, no more pressure, no more anxiety, from that quarter at least, until fall. Indy, says the man who for years has commanded the corps of six hundred ushers, "is spring tonic to me." I know what he means.

.   .   .   .

As with a great many contemporary experiences, the meaning of Indy is elusive because it won't fit familiar schemes of classification. Rationalists, trying to make sense of its competitive dimension, will conclude that news about it belongs on the sports page. But then Warner Wolf, the TV sports commentator, appalled by the destruction of Villeneuve and Smiley, argues that racing is not a sport at all and indignantly defames it as merely a thing about machines. Although there probably is a legitimate sport called "motor sport," indulged in largely by amateurs, Wolf is right in perceiving that what takes place at Indy is not really a sport. The essence of Indy is in its resemblance to other rituals in which wild, menacing, nonhuman things are tamed.

I am thinking of the rodeo and the bullfight. Subduing beasts that, unsubdued, would threaten man—that's the ritual enacted by rodeo, and, with some additional deepening of the irrational element, of the bullfight as well. Just as at Indy, you can get hurt trying to subdue wild horses, killed trying to dominate bulls. Virility, *cojones,* figure in each of these, as the little silver man indicates they do at Indy. Warner Wolf is also right when he notes that Indy is a thing about machines, but it's about machines only the way rodeos would be about broncos if no men were there to break them and bullfights about *toros* if no *toreros* were there to command them. Indy enacts the ritual taming and dominating of machines, emphasizing the crucial distinction between man and machine, the one soft and vulnerable but quick with courage and resource, the other hard and threatening but witless and unimaginative, stupid, indeed. The cars are at Indy so that men can be shown able to dominate them, and the wonder and glory of the dominators is the point. Indy is thus like a great Sunday-morning proclamation of the dignity of man, and no number of discarded chicken bones or trampled beer cans can change that. Like former Sunday morning rituals, Indy insists that people are worth being saved. If the machine should win, onlookers—sadists excepted—do not feel pleasure. The reasons the extinction of the space shuttle *Challenger* was so distressing are many, but one was certainly the spectacle of the machine, in that case, winning. Those aboard lost their lives not to something like a hurricane or an earthquake, but to a machine. The servant had suddenly turned master, and a vicious, violent master at that.

Do some people, regardless, come to see drivers killed? Probably, but as irrelevant a tiny number of the sick as those who enjoy seeing a bullfight ruined by a goring. If you see someone die at Indy, you are seeing that the machine has won, and that's opposed to everything the ritual is saying. No one enjoyed the moment in the 1987 race when a tire flew off one of the cars and killed a spectator. That was a victory for the machine, and like all such victories, it was messy and inartistic. A longtime student of the race, Sam Posey, seems to get the point when he considers the pleasure spectators take in identifying themselves with the driver-tamer of the machine. When things go wrong and the crowd sees a driver killed, he says, "They are terribly shocked and extremely depressed. They wish they had not been there." What the spectator wants to see is the machine crashing, disintegrating, wheels flying off, and in the end the man springing out and waving, "I'm okay." "Because that's the moment of the greatest thrill," says Posey. "That's when man has conquered the machine. The machine has bitten back, but the man jumps out laughing and therefore the spectator's dream of immortality is confirmed." Immortality: hence, value, and value much longer lasting than that conferred on the congeries of steel, aluminum, and rubber by the mere age of the machine.

I was at Indy during a week when every day brought worse news and more terrible images of people's limbs blown off in the South Atlantic, and perhaps the contrast between that spectacle and the Greatest Spectacle in Racing made Indy seem especially therapeutic. No one was hurt all the time I was there, the only injuries being sunburns and hangovers. I went looking for something mean, but what I found was not that at all. If Indy is in one sense about beer, in a deeper sense it's about milk, as the winning driver's victory refreshment suggests. A full-page ad in the official program, inserted by "Your Local Indiana Dairy Farmer," designated milk "the Drink of Champions" and noted that "over the past six years milk has powered the 'Fastest Rookie.' " Indy, the program also said, is "an American Tradition." It would be hard to find one ministering more comprehensively to the national spirit.

INDEX

ABOUT THE AUTHOR

Paul Fussell is Donald T. Regan Professor of English at the University of Pennsylvania and the author of *Class, The Boy Scout Handbook and Other Observations,* and many books on eighteenth-century and modern British culture. His book *The Great War and Modern Memory* won the National Book Award in 1976 as well as the National Book Critics Circle Award and the Ralph Waldo Emerson Award from Phi Beta Kappa. He has taught at Connecticut College, the University of Heidelberg and, for twenty-eight years, at Rutgers University. Mr. Fussell lives in Philadelphia.